CASH PAID FOR BUSINESS EXPENSE
Date
Chk. No.
NAME TO WHOM
Wages
Supplies
Freight Drayage
Expense
Orville Owen Reddest Born
Andrea Renoma Reddest
Virgie Gene Reddest
Leroy Clifford Reddest
Windell Jesse Reddest
Diana Electa Reddest
Eugene Thomas Reddest
Phyllis Ada Bull
Date
Name
Address
Clerk
Reg. No.
Account Forward
Dish Soap
gas
Oil
gas
total
$77.96
24
Your account stated to
or is found return at once.
Old age Money
I0821566
Mar 1960
year of 1887 only 3 family
in Potato Creek in
Rest the people ask
Hollow Head to move
at Potato Creek 1894

In honor of the Lakota people
and all the world's indigenous tribes!
Jon Willis

LEROY REDDEST'S CABIN,
LOST DOG CREEK.

EUGENE REDDEST (COMES OUT FIRST) AND
HIS ADOPTED DAUGHTER, VICTORIA.

LAGETTA ROSE POOR BEAR
AND HER NIECE.

1910 POSTCARD IMAGE OF REDDEST FAMILY RELATIONS BY J. A. MILLER, GORDON, NEBRASKA.

(LEFT TO RIGHT) SARAH TWO TAILS, FLORA BULL MAN, AND JESSIE TWO TAILS, CIRCA 1950.

I Stood

I stood beside an elder who
spoke words of life
I stood beside a man who
believed equality was right
I stood beside a woman
whose child was her life
I stood beside a man who
hated himself with passion
I stood beside a lover when
his life began
I stood beside my auntie
when her life had ended
I stood beside my family
when our world fell apart
I stood beside my heroes
we share the same heart

MONIQUE CLAYMORE
9TH GRADE

(LEFT TO RIGHT) JEREMY JONES,
(COWBOY) KELLY CEDAR FACE,
AND CHARLES MESTETH.

EUGENE WEARING A
COTTONWOOD WREATH.

POTATO CREEK.

res•er•va•tion (re-zər-vā-shən) noun (fifteenth century CE):
(1) an act of reserving something: an arrangement whereby something, such as a room or a seat, is booked or reserved in advance for a particular event; (2) something reserved, such as an area of public land set aside for occupation by North American Indians or Australian Aboriginals; (3) a qualification to an expression of agreement or approval; a doubt or misgiving; (4) a limiting condition.

SUNKA WAKAN NA WAKANYEJA AWICAGLIPI (TO BRING BACK THE HORSE AND CHILD), BATESLAND RACE DAY, FOURTH OF JULY POWWOW.

Views from the Reservation

A New Edition

by John Willis

with contributions from
the Oglala Lakota people and
an essay by Kent Nerburn

George F. Thompson Publishing
in association with the
American Land Publishing Project

THE MERRIVAL FAMILY'S
BUFFALO RANCH.

Dedicated to the memories of
Eugene Reddest, Tommy Crow, John Around Him,
Victoria Chipps, Maureen Last Horse,
Elden Ray (Sugar Ray) Marshall, Alma Richards,
Orville Reddest, Gwendolyn Bull Bear,
Victoria Jack Reddest, Rosie Has No Horse,
Kay Bull Bear, Leonard Little Finger,
Delores Yellow Bull, and John Red Feather, Jr.

And in loving memory of
Alan E. Willis, David P. Willis,
Ayla Miethner, and Meta Willis

NEW DEAL MURAL,
PINE RIDGE HIGH SCHOOL.

Contents

Mitakuye Oyasin (Opening Prayer)

Mitakuye Oyasin. These words, which are spoken at the beginning and end of Oglala Lakota prayers, translate as "All My Relations." Together they acknowledge that all things in life are related. This phrase is a conscious effort: to begin and end one's prayers with a deliberate reminder that all we do will affect all else and the balance within the world. This is the Sacred Hoop of Lakota life.

As part of the Sacred Hoop, all people living upon Mother Earth have an opportunity to take responsibility for individual actions and contribute to better collective actions by becoming more compassionate and generous to the earth and its soils and waters and sky and to all other living beings, striving to place great value on sharing heartfelt goodness with people from all walks of life in this time and in future generations. Such is the Spirit of Life.

So welcome to all who read this book, which is presented as an updated and expanded version of the original edition, published in 2010 and now sold out. It is an honor to share some perceptions of the Pine Ridge Reservation in South Dakota, and I am thankful for your willingness to reflect upon its content. There is so much one can share about Oglala Lakota culture, history, and contemporary life—so much value, beauty, and hardship that we all can learn and understand from the traditional ways, worldview, and life challenges of the Lakota people.

My hope with *Views from the Reservation: A New Edition* is to draw the reader in, to help raise awareness towards seeing the value of life on this and other reservations and to offer inspiration, even in the smallest ways, which may prove helpful towards achieving a more fair and just society for all. I do not in any way view this book as a comprehensive reference source but more as a compilation of visual and written imagery about wonderful people and a magnificent place.

Individual perceptions and actions can, at most, only begin to make a difference. The goal with the book is not to create assimilation into Lakota society but to honor and support the culture, as we would want others to respect our own. I cannot express enough gratitude to the late Eugene Reddest, his extended family members, and the other Lakota people I have come to know since my first visit in 1992, for welcoming me on that and every subsequent visit and for dramatically affecting my life. With this book I also honor the ancestors.

Even as I may feel as much at home and at peace on Lakota land as anywhere, I am an outsider, no matter how many times I visit. Even as I may sense the heartbeat of the reservation through its land and people, I do not presume to be able to do more than scratch the surface in my photographic work. No one person can comprehend the realities of Pine Ridge and the Lakota people in a finite way, especially for a non-native. And so I am very thankful for the other voices in this book—from Kent Nerburn to the many Lakota people—who provide additional insights and views of this special culture and place. They have taught me much—especially important is the belief that all things are related and require our humble respect.

When thinking of the Pine Ridge Reservation, what do people imagine? What are the preconceived notions that outsiders carry about the place, the people, the culture, and their way of life? Pine Ridge is the Oglala Lakota Tribe's home, a territory that traditionally covered a large geographic area, from Minnesota west to the sacred Black Hills (*Paha Sapa*) of southwestern South Dakota and eastern Wyoming. Today, the reservation has been reduced to approximately fifty by 100 miles. Both outsiders and native peoples know of Hollywood's representation of the "American Indian" culture. So often it has been based on the Lakota and other indigenous tribes of the Great Plains and Interior West.

Most of us have heard of the problems with alcoholism, drugs, poverty, suicide, and gangs on the reservations, of the brutal massacre at Wounded Knee in 1890, of the occupation of Wounded Knee by the American Indian Movement and its supporters in 1973, and of the Standing Rock Lakota Tribe's leadership in resisting in 2016–2017 the location of the Dakota Access Pipeline (DAPL) through its sacred and sovereign lands, including burial grounds, and to direct attention to renewable energy as an alternative to oil and natural gas. But how much do most outsiders really know of Lakota land and life?

I am forever thankful that I have come to gain friendship with many Lakota people and to know many as a family. This book is intended to be a *wopila* (a gift) for them and for all Lakota people, for all they have given me through who they are and for their willingness to be so welcoming. I feel deeply indebted to them for reminding me what is truly important in life. It is not oil. It is not uranium. It is not natural gas. It is land and sky and water and people and other creatures living harmoniously together as a community.

May life in every way and form become easier for the Lakota people as they work hard to hold on to their culture and traditional ways that inspire pride and generate lasting dignity from one generation to the next. That is my prayer.

Mitakuye Oyasin
John Willis

Views from the Reservation

Lakota Commandments

Oneness with *Tunkasila*, loving one another unconditionally.
Respect for all beings.
Generosity, kindness, and assistance wherever needed.
Truth and honesty, live it at all times.
Balance, do what you know to be right.
Physical, keep in check the well-being of mind and body.
Harmony, treat the earth well and all that dwell thereon.
Responsibility, take full control of your actions.
Humility, dedicate a share of your efforts to greater good.
Unity, working together for the benefit of all mankind with patience.

These are the rules I live by, taught to me by the elders.

ALMA RICHARDS, ELDER

AERIAL VIEW OF A PRAIRIE DOG COLONY.

TOMMY CROW,
KANGI HOKSILA (CROW BOY).

MOUNT RUSHMORE NATIONAL MONUMENT, WHERE THE FACES OF FOUR U.S. PRESIDENTS ARE CARVED OR, AS MANY NATIVE PEOPLE SAY, SCARRED INTO THE SACRED BLACK HILLS (*PAHA SAPA*).

(LEFT TO RIGHT) ANNA DIAZ AND ASHLEY PHELPS, ALLEN COMMUNITY POWWOW.

Belong . . .

That's where I want to be someday.
I would like to belong.
Belong where I go,
Belong where I live.
Where I stay,
I want to belong.
Belong because it is not mine, but our domain,
Belong to my territory
And in my territory I shall remain.
No arguments,
No hesitations.
I want to belong,
Belong to this Great Nation.

LISA MARIE PALMIER
11TH GRADE

TATANKA (BISON).

VICTORIA CHIPPS, OF THE HORN CHIPPS LINEAGE OF MEDICINE MEN, ON HER NINETIETH BIRTHDAY WITH HER GREAT-GRANDDAUGHTER.

ESTHER MOVES CAMP
PRAYING TO THE SUN
DANCE TREE A DAY AFTER
THE CEREMONY ENDED.
USED BY PERMISION.

EUGENE PREPARING THE *C'ANUPA* (SACRED PIPE) BEFORE THE *INIPI* (SWEAT LODGE) CERMEONY. USED BY PERMISSION.

The Hero in Me

She smiles, she laughs, she hurts,
She cries.
She holds it all deep inside.
She lives, she flies, she soars,
She dies.
She is the one I idolize.
She loves, she gives, she cares.
She is
The one I will someday
Be—
A hero, a mother, a child, a soul,
The woman inside of me.

ISABELLE BRAVEHEART
10TH GRADE

ALLEN COMMUNITY
POWWOW.

EUGENE AND HIS SON, LEROY, LOOKING FOR *TIMPSILA* (WILD TURNIP ROOT), A TRADITIONAL INGREDIENT USED IN SOUPS AND OTHER FOODS.

BUREAU OF INDIAN AFFAIRS
(BIA) ROUTE 18.

TIMPSILA
(WILD TURNIP ROOT).

TONY TELLING HARD STORIES OF RAISING CHILDREN WHILE BEING OUT OF WORK.

ELLEN HOLLOW HEAD'S
SWEAT LODGE (*INIPI)* BEFORE
THE *INIPI* CEREMONY.
USED BY PERMISSION.

EUGENE LEAVING THE
INIPI (SWEAT LODGE),
HIS CHURCH WHERE HE
WOULD GO TO PRAY,
HEAL, AND HELP OTHERS.
USED BY PERMISSION.

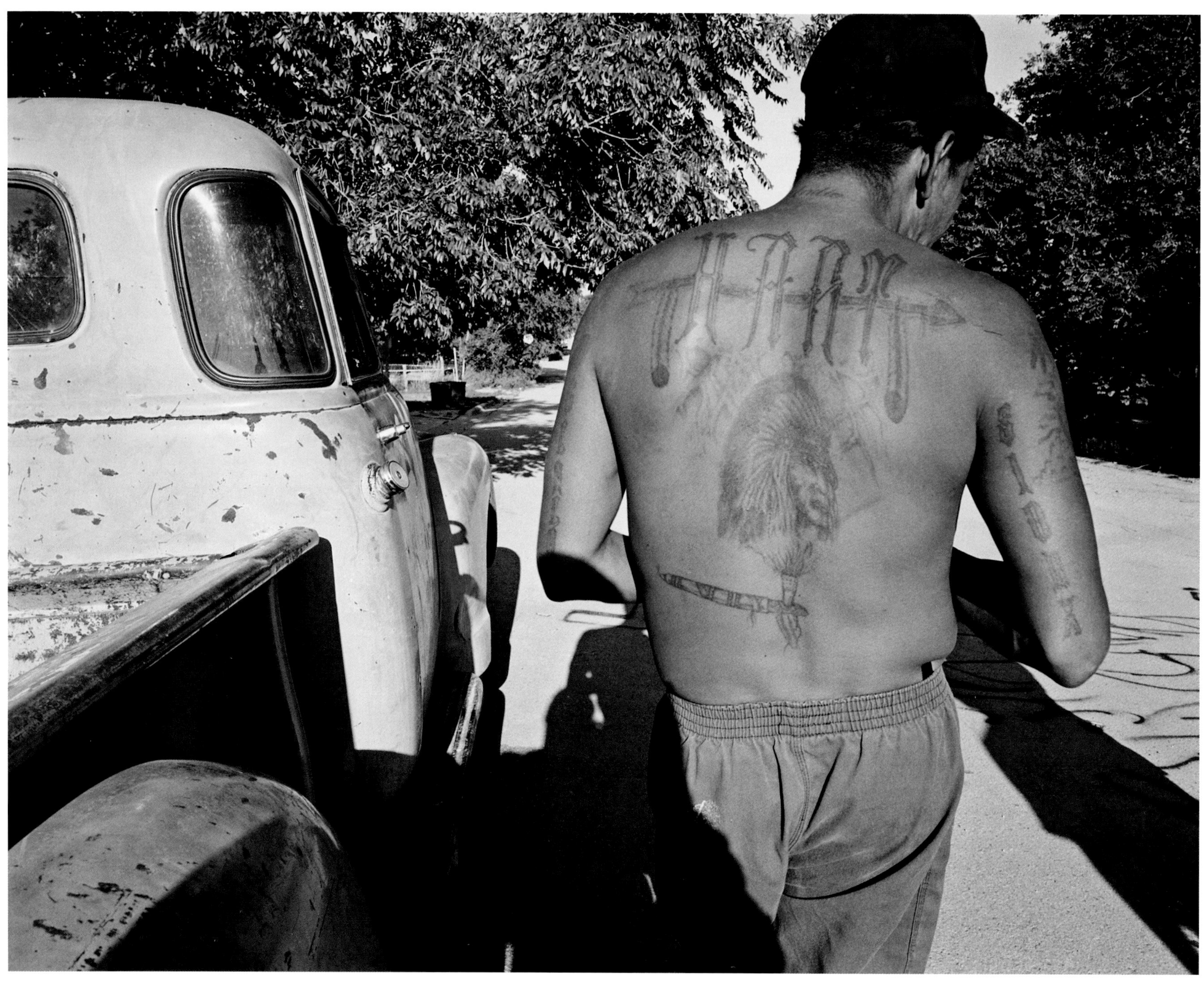

DOING CHORES FOR THE
COMMUNITY WHILE ON
WORK FURLOUGH FROM
THE TRIBAL JAIL.

EAST PINE RIDGE.

BIA HOUSING IN 2006.

BIA HOUSING IN 2007.

VICTORIA ON HER
NINETIETH BIRTHDAY.

Be Thankful

You have to say a prayer of Thanksgiving.
You have to be thankful.

Otherwise it's like a house without windows.
It's dark.

In the morning when you wake up from a good night's sleep, you open your eyes and you see the light.
Say a prayer of thanksgiving before you get up.
Thank you. Thank you *Tunkasila* for another day.

VICTORIA CHIPPS, ELDER

The Four Sacred Things

I told you about it,
The four sacred things
That we are supposed to remember.

The Sun
The Moon
The Thunder Beings
And the Stone People.

Umpewi is the sun.
Hanhewi is the moon.
Wakinyan oyate is the Thunder Beings
And *inyan oyate* is the stone people.

I tell people to remember
That these four are forever sacred.

VICTORIA CHIPPS, ELDER

GARY GOOD VOICE ELK
AT EUGENE'S FUNERAL.

BIA ROUTE 44.

I am from . . .

I am from potato salad and deep-fried chicken
From Barbie dolls and chokecherry pickin'
I am from sleeping outside under the stars
From playing freeze tag on old junk cars
I am from eating cereal and eggs in the morning
From school every week that got really boring
I am Super Nintendo and Nintendo 64
From flowered dresses and tights that are always torn
From climbing trees and scraped-up knees
From playing with puppies infested with fleas
Yes I'm from all these things, that's me
Because I'm from the beautiful country

SAMANTHA RED FEATHER
12TH GRADE

Hold Your Breath

Breathe. Focus. Everything rides on this.
Don't mess up. One thing wrong and there goes your future.
Deep breath.
INHALE.
Everyone knows you are trying, don't let them down. You have to
be better than the next guy. Don't mess up. Don't mess up. Don't
mess up! This is so important. You'll never amount to anything
if you don't get this right, you HAVE to. It's too big for you to
goof off. If you fail at this, you fail at life. People will only re-
member you for this one thing. Give them something to remember.
Don't mess up. Focus. Don't let them down.
Exhale.

AMANDELINE ECOFFEY
12TH GRADE

PINE RIDGE.

MICHELLE GOINGS
AND FAMILY.

FATHER AND SON.

VERN SITTING BEAR,
A HOOP DANCER, ON
A SUNDAY MORNING.

405 INIPI ROAD.

WHITE CLAY DAM.

OGLALA.

In the Struggle, We Stand

In the struggle we stand, shields and shawls
It's in this struggle great duty calls
It's a duty to Oyate, a duty to the people
Use your head Sitting Bull said
Find what's lost, move us ahead
Cause there's more to history
Than what meets the book
There's a blizzard blowing hard
And it's 100 degrees
In the struggle we stand kin to kin
Struggle to stand through strength from within
Look back to where and why, when and how
Hold on to what's dear, *c'anupa* in our hearts
Families rent asunder, cultures ripped apart
In the struggle we stand, seven generations thence
Diplomas and degrees and learned and smart
We talk and we read and glean from past days
We find where we are and where we've been
In the struggle we stand

LAVELLE WARRIOR
9TH GRADE

EDNA APPLE.

EARLY MORNING AT
POKER JOE AND ABBY
MERRIVAL'S HOME.

EDDIE GALE, RETIRED
RODEO BULL RIDER.

CHECKING THE LAUNDRY.

EDDIE WALKING ON
WITT ROAD, PINE RIDGE.

BRINGING HOME THE
MONTHLY COMMODITIES.

VERN SITTING BEAR AND
HIS NIECE'S PET WOLF.

ALLEN COMMUNITY HOUSING.

EUGENE AT HOME.

ORVILLE REDDEST.

NEW YEAR'S DAY,
DUANE REDDEST'S HOME,
LOST DOG CREEK.

THE NO FLESH ROAD.

BIA ROUTE 120.

Some Place

The grass is green
The wind is blowing
Everything comes together perfectly
Tall are the trees
High is the sky
Onward the horse rides
However long it takes
Rides on to destiny . . . .

PHILLIP CLARKE
10TH GRADE

BATESLAND RACE DAY,
FOURTH OF JULY POWWOW.

WATER TOWER,
SHARPS CORNER.

THE MASS GRAVESITE AT
WOUNDED KNEE FROM
THE MASSACRE OF 1890.

SHARPS CORNER.

A RESERVATION RESPONSE TO THE U.S. PRESIDENTIAL CAMPAIGN OF 2004. THE SENTIMENT AGAINST REPUBLICANS REMAINS TRUE FOR MOST LAKOTA PEOPLE TODAY.

A VETERAN'S PROTEST TO
THE TREATMENT OF MUSLIMS
AFTER 9/11/2001.

SECURITY SHACK FOR A SUN DANCE TO KEEP OUT UNWANTED VISITORS.

VETERAN'S HONOR GUARD
AT THE GRADUATION
POWWOW, OGLALA
LAKOTA COLLEGE.

THE FUNERAL OF U.S. MARINE CORPORAL BRETT LUNDSTROM, *WANBLI ISNALA* (LONE EAGLE), WHO WAS KILLED IN ACTION IN 2006 WHILE SERVING IN IRAQ.

A FUTURE SUN DANCE SITE.

Listening for the Meadowlark's Song

BY KENT NERBURN

I'm standing on a windswept ridge, high above the dusty town of Kyle, South Dakota, in the center of the Pine Ridge Lakota Reservation. The hills roll away from me in endless profusion—green rhythms of land stretching to an infinite horizon like the waves on a rolling sea.

In a few months, the spring rains will cease, and all this will be brown. The wind will burn with a dragon's breath, and the grasses will hiss and rattle and cut my feet as I walk. Crickets will lurch against me, and I will have to avoid the shadows of the low, ground-hugging rocks for fear of rattlesnakes.

I will not want to be here then, for I'm not good with waterless places. But it's a joy to be here now, with an azure blue sky vaulting overhead and tens of thousands of cottonball clouds rolling like kittens toward the endless horizon.

This is magical land, this Pine Ridge Reservation: a mystical land that hypnotizes the eye and stills the heart. The hills echo with the memory of long-departed seas; outcroppings of rocks jut like bone through flesh. In the far distance, a solitary volcanic cone stands sentinel over the rolling landscape. I stand in the center: insignificant, absorbed, less knower than known, a part of something too large to be fathomed and understood. The whole landscape feels ancient and alive.

I remember standing on a similar hill not many miles from here in the midst of deep summer more than a decade ago. The nourishing spring rains had long departed, and only momentary squalls graced the land with moisture. It was late afternoon, and the sky had turned a darkening gray. Beyond the horizon, dim light flashed like explosions in a distant room. Thunder grumbled in the distance.

I had never felt a landscape so alive with animal presence. The storm seemed palpable and breathing. It moved as if searching. When it passed, I felt like I had been spared. I was humbled and filled with gratitude.

The Lakota people who live here take such feelings for granted, just as they take for granted the fierce winter winds that bury the roads in snow and cut the skin like glass and the crenellated sandstone menhirs and dolmens that stand like lunar Cambodian temples in the outcroppings of badlands that punctuate these prairie lands.

The animal presence of the land is no surprise to them, just as it has been no surprise to their grandparents and their grandparents' grandparents going back to the time when their people were driven here by the incursion of European settlers farther east. In those days, the Lakota were a more woodland people; their brothers and sisters, the Dakota, still are. But, once on this land, their history took root, and their character was formed. They are now of this land, and this land is of them. They are alive to the palpable presence of life in every tree that stands solitary on a lonely hillside, aware of meaning in the soarings of the red-tailed hawk and the shift in the direction of the wind.

What is so astonishing to an outsider like me is the way in which this awareness of a pervasive presence of spirit permeates the lives of the people who live here. I recall sitting with a ninety-two-year-old man in a local café. He wore an old crumpled fishing cap and a long-sleeved white shirt buttoned at the wrists. His skin was as brown and burnished as the land. He was diligently occupied in snapping his French fries in half and rubbing the pieces together to divest them of their salt.

"My grandmother used to talk to the meadowlarks," he told me. "They would sit on the fence posts as she hung out the clothes, and she would sometimes laugh and say things to them. I remember one day she got angry and threw a rock at one of them. I heard her scolding it as it flew away. A little neighbor baby died the next day. I guess she didn't like hearing what the meadowlark had to say."

And it is not only the elders who have such a sensibility. Not long ago I was standing outside the library of the Oglala Lakota College, talking with a woman whose job it is to drive the back roads from community to community, bringing books to outreach programs that have no libraries. She is a professional woman, well-skilled in the ways of administration. Her conversation is peppered with phrases like "allocation of resources" and "maximizing utilization." She has held responsible positions in non-profit organizations throughout the West in settings both urban and rural.

We were staring at the crumpled fender and broken headlight of her car.

"A deer hit," she said.

"Well, the deer must have gotten the worst of it," I responded, trying to make light of a difficult situation.

Her face darkened imperceptibly—just a shadow, like a momentary darkening of these hilltops when the sun passes behind a cloud. "It wasn't a normal deer," she said and walked back into the office.

Of such understanding is life here made: Meadowlarks tell stories, hawks bring messages, a deer jumping in front of your car is more than a mere accident. All is connected; all has meaning. The linear, rational world from which we outsiders come feels thin and reedy.

Perhaps this is why so many non-native seekers are drawn here. The paucity of our spiritual experience—in which time is linear and a hard demarcation exists between the sacred and the ordinary—is obliterated.

Here, spiritual meaning inheres in every object and is present in every moment. Here, even the most ordinary and debased human activity is alive with spiritual portent and presence.

One evening a few years ago, I decided to drive to Whiteclay, a cruel little unincorporated town just across the border into Nebraska, two miles south of the reservation. Whiteclay is only two blocks long, with a few ramshackle storefronts and cinder-block buildings flanking the two-lane highway (NE 87) that bisects the town.

Historically, Whiteclay has existed for only one main reason: to sell alcohol to the reservation, where alcohol is illegal. As of the last U.S. Census (2010), the population of Whiteclay was twenty-two. Its story began in 1904, when a few trading posts were established by white merchants who began to sell alcohol to their Lakota neighbors. In 2016, three stores were selling around 11,000 cans and bottles of beer a day, and the annual take for liquor sales was nearly $4,000,000. All that changed on September 29, 2017, when the Nebraska Supreme Court banned beer sales in Whiteclay, ending, at least for now, a long-standing pipeline of alcohol to the reservation.

Even today, with the ban on alcohol, Whiteclay is an uncomfortable place to go at night. The few sodium lights seem ghostly in the vast prairie darkness. Shadowy figures huddle in the doorways. Bodies lie slumped on the ground, passed out in an alcoholic stupor. Starving dogs peer out through the darkness, and trash piles up against the corners of buildings. You sense instinctively that no good things happen here, and you want to get through town as quickly as possible.

I wanted to see Whiteclay at night. I wanted to sense its presence for myself. This was before the ban on beer. So I stopped at one of the three existing liquor stores under the guise of getting a bottle of water. It was no typical liquor store, with bottles lined on shelves along the walls; merely a small waiting area in a crude cement-block building where you stand until the young white man in the baseball cap who is working behind the counter brings your purchased bottle from behind a protective screen.

There was one other man in the waiting area. He was Lakota, well over six feet tall, with deep-set dark eyes that balanced on the knife edge between violence and tragedy. He watched me closely as I entered.

I had expected to be asked for money—the shadowy figures that congregate in the darkness are waiting for just such a passerby as me—and I was prepared to offer something for the privilege of a human encounter, however bleak and tawdry.

The Lakota man did as all drunken panhandlers do—he reached out his hand in greeting and told me his name. His whole body was ravaged by alcohol, and he could barely speak. "I see you got a good spirit," he slurred.

He held my hand loosely but firmly; he was not about to let me get away.

"I can tell these things. My uncle was a medicine man."

He leaned closer. His breath was rotten, and his face was covered with sweat.

"You think I'm just a drunk," he said, the violence moving closer to the surface. "I've done Sun Dance. I got eagle feathers." He almost fell over as he spoke.

Then he softened. "Say," he said, still holding my hand firmly in his. "You wouldn't have a couple quarters to help a brother, would you?"

I reached in my pocket with my free hand and pulled out a dollar bill.

"I hate to give money to someone who's destroying himself," I said. "But I appreciate your conversation, and I honor your right to do what you want with your life."

He took the dollar and looked directly in my eyes—something that Indian people are not wont to do.

"I'm going to read about you in the *Bible* tomorrow," he said. The violence had receded, and the tragedy was welling to the surface.

"I hope it's going to be something good," I answered.

He looked at the dollar and then back at me. "'I was thirsty, and you gave me to drink.' Isn't that what Jesus wants?" His eyes glistened with tears. His hand loosened around mine, and he gently and quietly released me from his grip. Outside, his friends were gathered in the darkness, waiting for a new bottle. We stayed connected for a moment, looking into each other's eyes. Then I walked out into the star-filled night.

Under ordinary circumstances I would say it was just another encounter with a drunk who used religion as a tool of panhandling. But such was not the case. Even in his stupor, this man was alive to spiritual power and connection. That it was a confused cacophony of Lakota and Christian voices made it all the more poignant.

I drove away from Whiteclay filled with disquiet. Here was another man, all too willing to talk about the power of spirit, even though it had been decayed into an alcoholic petition for drink. In him had been embodied the three forces that do battle for the contemporary Lakota soul: drugs and alcohol, the Christian church, and the traditional beliefs and practices.

HISTORY WALK: 500 YEARS OF MAKING AMERICA GREAT. INK AND COLORED PENCIL ON 1938 LEDGER PAPER: 17.0" X 11.75" (2010).

Each has power. Each is a way to look beyond the grinding and inescapable poverty—a way to penetrate into a deeper realm and find a meaning that is greater than the physical and economic struggles of the world around them.

I thought of the old man with his French fries and a darker part of our encounter that day in the café. He was recounting his time as a boy in the boarding schools, where he had been sent as part of the U.S. government policy to "kill the Indian and save the man." His time there had been tough, with beatings and deprivations and separation from his family and physical abuse for speaking his own language.

I listened respectfully as he unburdened himself about whippings and humiliations and being locked in dark closets for hours at a time. As we prepared to part he looked down and said so softly that I could barely hear, "I learned. I can speak good English. I became a Christian. But I am no longer myself. I am someone else."

This, I thought, is what was contained in that complex, unnerving expression of tragedy and violence in the eyes of my drunken friend in Whiteclay. He was no longer himself. The residue of the old spiritual knowledge—the knowledge that is everywhere in the winds and the hills and the spirit of this land—had been lost to him, tamped down by a Christianity he could not fully embrace and obliterated by the alcohol that allows him to forget what it is that he cannot fully remember.

"I am no longer myself. I am someone else."

This is the struggle that the Lakota people face. This is the dark legacy that we non-native Americans must acknowledge.

We have, by our intrusion onto the land they believe the Creator has given them for their own, taken their once-proud culture and obliterated it with boarding schools and outing programs, where children were taken away from their families and placed in non-Indian homes to learn "civilized" ways; where the language was ripped from their lips by threats of punishment, leaving the truths of their elders and the subtleties of their beliefs and their land insusceptible to expression by the flat, analytical, subject-object constructions of English; where their ways of living and sharing and honoring the rhythms of the seasons were hammered into the square-cornered, mercantile dross of nine-to-five capitalism. Alcohol, that biological and cultural conundrum that resists all attempts at solutionship, eats like a disease at the very core of reservation life, and Christianity, the spear point of a cultural thrust that includes everything from individualism to capitalism, pushes defiantly against the quiet, personal native beliefs and practices that are the very center of Lakota life and the Lakota way of being.

They are no longer themselves; they are someone else. And the struggle of their lives is to reclaim who they once were while making peace with the people they have become.

I drove back to Pine Ridge through the deep Dakota darkness. I did not sleep well, and I was filled with something close to shame.

The silence on this hill is overwhelming. It is a noisy silence, filled with activity and life. Grasses rustle; insects flutter and buzz; the wind ebbs and flows like the soughing of the sea.

Far below me Kyle sits in a vast bowl of land. It is a small and ragged outpost, diminished and miniature in this great, rolling landscape. It has none of the implied sense of order that I associate with American towns, even small, rural enclaves out here in the High Plains. Few streets go off at right angles; no trees shade the yards and roadways. It is little more than a momentary widening of the thin ribbon of highway that cuts singular through the hills.

A few prefabricated steel buildings sit back from the main road on dusty, gravel pull-offs. The Little Wound School sits brick and solid on a small apron of asphalt. Small, rectangular, government-issue houses in their clapboard sameness flank several side streets that fade off into fields. Abandoned chairs and couches sit half-hidden in the weeds; cars rest on cement blocks or lie turned on their sides, baked and rusted from years in the hot summer sun. Here and there a small dog yips and barks at the end of a too-short chain, and freshly washed clothes flap like flags of defiance in the noonday sun.

It feels like poverty, and it is. The Pine Ridge Reservation is one of the poorest places in all the Americas. In 2010, the typical family lived on less than $4,000 a year; in 2018, it was $7,773. An average of eleven people live in each house, and many of those houses are without plumbing and running water. As in all such places, something of human initiative is lost, and that which seems obvious is left unaddressed—junk cars, trash blowing in the streets, burned-out houses covered with graffiti. It challenges, even offends, sensibilities raised on cleanliness and order.

But poverty is a relative term, and cleanliness and order are in the eye of the beholder. To a European accustomed to the manicured passageways of the Schwarzwald, the unkempt understories of our American forests, with their seedlings and deadfall and impassable bramble, are a chaos of disorder. To the Lakota, the poverty of everyday life, with its attendant urban landscape of abandonments and half-efforts, is as unremarkable as that tangled forest understory and as much a part of daily life as the endless sprawl of asphalt parking lots and strip malls are to those who live in the more affluent

HOUSING REMNANTS, POTATO CREEK.

corners of metropolitan America. The spaces and places that surround us are simply the way they are, and we live our lives around them, trying to find goodness and order as best we can within the lives we are given.

This is not to say that the poverty goes unnoticed or does not impact the people. When each day is a struggle and making it from paycheck to paycheck—if, indeed, there is a paycheck—is a constant challenge, your life is ground downward with an inexorable force.

Most of us can only dimly imagine what it is to run out of heating oil in mid-December and be facing a January of twenty-below-zero temperatures and forty-mile-an-hour winds without heat; or to walk to a school bus stop in those same temperatures with gloves with no fingers and only a thin jacket as protection from the cutting edge of the winds.

We cannot imagine what it is to have the few local stores stocked with the worst produce that the distributor has to offer or to have the simplest services we take for granted—doctors, dentists, clothing stores, pharmacies—sometimes a hundred miles away.

I remember sitting with a woman in the kitchen of her small, tarpaper house, three miles back into the hills on a rutted, barely passable road. The house had been built in stages with scavenged materials, and it barely kept out the incessant winter winds. Papers were strewn on every surface, and the wall behind her was stacked with canned goods. Her meal of macaroni and cheese was bubbling on the stove.

She lives alone; her husband died some thirty years ago. Her son is her pride and joy, and she longs for his visits. He is a good son. But the "brown bottle" got him, then harder drugs, and he committed a crime off the reservation. For the last several years he has been in and out of prison. He now lives in Rapid City, more than two hours by car from the family home on the reservation.

"Every time I get out, Momma," he tells her, "I try to get a job, but no one will hire me. I'm an Indian and a con. They think I'm a bad man."

He would come back to the reservation, he says, but it's more than 100 miles to Rapid City, and he must go there twice a week for drug testing. Even on the good days there is little money for gas, the old car is fragile, and the roads are rutted and difficult. In snow and icy weather, they are impassable. To miss a test is to violate parole. It isn't worth the risk. "So I keep trying, but, jeez, it's hard."

The story is so common as to seem ordinary: cars that break down; houses that can't keep out the cold; illnesses that are left untreated; medicines that are left unpurchased. Lives are controlled by U.S. government regulations that are ever-changing and impossible to follow.

To the outside world this life seems unfathomable. Except to those of us who labor under the delusion that "Indians" get wealthy from casino money or that their poverty is nothing more than the logical consequence of indolence, the plight of these people is heartbreaking.

Many outsiders, touched by this plight, come to the reservation to do what they can. On any given day church groups from around the country can be found repairing houses or constructing school buildings or delivering clothes and canned goods by the vanload to the various church and social-service agencies on the reservation.

Mostly, folks on the reservation accept these visitors with good graces. They are pleased to receive needed assistance in a place where official unemployment historically lingers around seventy percent, and they appreciate the good-heartedness of those who give so freely of their time and money.

But their acceptance is not without its dark side. One young man, sitting on a stoop, watched the string of volunteers come out of the local store and get in their rented cars and church vans. "I hope they brought some green paint this year," he says. "I'm getting tired of living in a yellow house." It is only half a joke, and in its nuances and ambiguities it speaks volumes.

Then there is the woman who struggles to find the words not to sound ungrateful. "It's hard to take someone else's used clothes," she says. "In our tradition, we always give the best. We would never think of giving something we no longer wanted as a gift to someone else."

I understand their ambivalence, and I share it. For the Lakota are heir to centuries of cultural suppression. They need assistance, they deserve assistance, and, in all fairness, they are owed assistance. But they know, and we know, that the assistance reinforces their victimhood and underscores their dependency. For, no matter how it is offered, it still feels patronizing, just as the used clothes, no matter how well-laundered and folded, speak of charity rather than valuing, just as the dollar offered to the drunk feels more like an act of noblesse oblige or charity than an honoring of the spirit of the man to whom it was given.

The wind is picking up now. It is a fresh and cleansing wind, moving with a lyrical hand across the hills. The birdsong waxes and wanes with the intensity of the gusts—a strange correlation I can neither understand nor deny. Everything has the rhythm of breath: the hills and swales that stretch to the distant horizon, the winds rising and falling, the sweeping movements of the clouds as they form and disband in the arching blue sky.

SARAH GHOST BEAR, NO FLESH ROAD.

I look down for a moment from the hypnotic rhythm of the sky and land. At my feet are hundreds of white flowers poking through the sharp and brittle grasses. Insects dance and swirl around my head. The sweet warble of a meadowlark carves a sharp, flutelike line through the chanting of the winds.

It is easy be overwhelmed by the vast grandeur of this landscape and to ignore the profusion of intimacies that teem with vibrancy and life, just as it is easy to be overwhelmed by the great historical and social injustices done to the Lakota people, while overlooking the moments of hope and possibility that spring forth everywhere on the reservation.

On the door inside the general store far below me in Kyle is a poster entreating Lakota speakers to speak only the Lakota language to children from the time of their birth until they enter school, so the language, and the way it teaches one to see the world, will once again take root and flourish. In each of the Pine Ridge communities, so widely separated from each other in this broad rolling landscape, a community center provides computers and a rotating selection of books brought in from the central library at Lakota Oglala College at Kyle. The college and its outreach campuses at all the small villages on the reservation promote research into diabetes and wind power, train nurses and teachers, and send more than 100 graduates into the community and wider world every year. KILI radio, "The Voice of the Lakota Nation," connects the isolated homes and separate communities with everything from traditional powwow music to weather reports, announcements about birthdays and events, and documentaries about Indian culture and history.

And beneath even these broader social actions are the quiet, private gestures and efforts: the man who collects broken bicycles and fixes them for the children of the community; the descendant of Big Foot, the chief slaughtered by the soldiers at Wounded Knee, who has quietly started a school, without governmental assistance, that teaches the children through immersion in the Lakota language; and the family that trains the local children in the traditional ways of Lakota horsemanship. Like the white flowers beneath my feet, these blooms sprout everywhere on the reservation, too often unnoticed by those intent only upon seeing the broad sweep of poverty and historical injustice.

But it is neither the poverty nor the possibility that draws me to this place, nor is it some need for cultural atonement or personal redemption. The heart of the Lakota people draws me to this place.

Come with me, for a moment, to the home of the woman who makes star quilts for giveaways on the reservation. The giveaway is the traditional practice of offering gifts to people of significance at moments of passage or accomplishment in a person's life. The star quilt is the most honored gift that can be offered—the contemporary equivalent of the buffalo robe. To bestow it on someone is a sign of the greatest honor and respect.

Though hobbled by arthritis, this quiet woman with her gentle smile works to make sure that there are always enough star quilts available to give away at birthdays, graduations, marriages, memorial services, and every other ceremonial occasion where a gift of significance is required.

Then travel to a memorial service for the departed and see a 250-gallon watering trough filled with buffalo soup and five tables covered with foods of every sort. Watch as everyone is fed until they can eat no more, and the rest is placed in Tupperware containers for those who have nothing to eat at home. See the strangers stop and be welcomed, because their presence is an honor. Watch the family of the deceased, often so poor themselves that they live without running water and food enough to fill their table, give gifts to everyone in attendance, from star quilts to the possessions of the deceased, to small presents purchased at dollar stores.

Watch these things and realize that you are hearing the echo of the great Lakota value of *wacantognaka*, or generosity, and that it lives today, as surely as it did in the days of Crazy Horse and Sitting Bull.

Or travel to the Sun Dance, that most sacred of Lakota rituals, where, after days of fasting, young men and women—some piercing their flesh with eagle bones—tie themselves to the sacred cottonwood tree and dance without food or drink for four days and nights in sacrifice for their people. See this and know that you are in the presence of the traditional Lakota value of *wacintaka*, or fortitude, and that it, too, is still alive in the everyday life of the people on Pine Ridge.

Or see the young children, barely old enough to walk, proudly wearing their jingle dresses and moccasins and mimicking the dance steps of their parents as they move around the powwow ring; or accept the offer to enter a sweat lodge—the *inipi*—and give yourself over to the stifling darkness, where the sense of self is annihilated and the body and spirit are cleansed and purified in an ancient ritual that echoes the experience of birth and death.

Everywhere you look these fundamental Lakota values are alive and in flower: the practice of silence and self-control; the selfless generosity; the humility that keeps them from ever praising themselves or extolling their own accomplishments; the valuing of the knowledge of elders. These and so many others echo up from the Lakota past and give Lakota life a groundedness and grace that cannot be suppressed by poverty or pathology.

HONORING THE LIFE OF U.S. MARINE CORPORAL BRETT LUNDSTROM, WHO WAS KILLED IN ACTION IN FALLUJAH, IRAQ.

But, more than that, they give life a continuity. Every child feels the presence of Sitting Bull and Red Cloud, every soldier the memory of Crazy Horse.

This morning I passed a dilapidated trailer set back in a dusty field. Old appliances lay scattered in the weeds. Carcasses of abandoned cars sat canted on cement blocks. At first glance it seemed but one more junk-strewn, poverty-stricken residence, reflective of the indifference and half-efforts that so confound American middle-class sensibilities. But above the front door, waving proudly in the morning breeze, were an American flag and the black and white memorial flag of the MIAs and POWs. This was the home of a veteran, and those flags bespoke not poverty but pride.

Outsiders are always confounded by this pride with which Lakota men and women will serve a government that has systematically stolen their land, obliterated their culture, and relegated them to a Third World status in one of the richest countries in the world.

We impute their motives to economics—that there are few other routes out of the poverty and economic hardship of reservation life. But this does not explain the convoy of veterans who drove the 100-plus miles to the Rapid City airport to meet the casket of a young soldier killed in Iraq in the line of duty, or the 150 cars that waited at the reservation border to honor the young man's return, or the hundreds of people who lined the side of the road in silent witness as the casket passed. It does not explain the honoring of veterans at the powwows or the wall of photos of reservation veterans that encircles the library of Oglala Lakota College.

These actions, these gestures, go far beyond the simple explanation of economics. They go to the heart of the Lakota belief in service to others. Ohiyesa, the great native thinker who was part of the Lakota's sister tribe, the Dakota, spoke of this belief when he said that he who chooses the route of the warrior "sets no price upon either his property or his labor. His generosity is limited only by his strength. He regards it as an honor to be selected for a difficult or dangerous service and would think it a shame to ask for any other reward..."

This belief in the sacredness of service makes Lakota men and women so willing to don the uniform of the U.S. military and to risk their lives in service of the nation. To them, it is a gift to their people and to all other First Nation peoples throughout America; and, in its giving, it is honored and valued by all those who remain behind.

The clouds are gathering now. The wind has turned chill, presaging rain. I walk down the trail and get into my car. The road before me is rough, little more than a rude clay path. It intrudes upon the land no more than a stream or rivulet—a momentary fixing of the attention before the eye scans outward to the vast expanse of horizon that mirrors the curvature of Earth.

It is easy to see how the past remains alive for the Lakota people. Except for this road, so small and insignificant, little is changed from the days when their ancestors rode free across these hills, unburdened by the intrusion of an alien and dominating culture and the weight of its harsh history.

It is hard to explain this presence of the past to those who come from a world fixated on individual accomplishment and focused on the future, hard to communicate to those weaned on notions of progress and human advancement. But to stand on this land is, for a moment, to understand, if only dimly, how a child can be raised to serve the memory of his or her ancestors, how a woman can willingly embrace the ways of her tradition and subsume her individuality into the good of the collectivity. For there are ghosts here, and memories, and feeling their presence and doing them honor is as natural as feeling the pulsating presence of life in a thunderstorm or sensing the outlines of a message in a meadowlark's song.

Around a decade ago, during a dangerous dry spell, I was sitting on an old oil drum outside a store in Pine Ridge, reading the newspaper. The day was hot and dusty; the talk of drought was everywhere. Ranchers were trucking barrels of water out to their livestock. Farms in the eastern part of the state were in danger of losing their irrigation. The great Missouri River (*Mni Sose*), "the bringer of life," was taxed to its limits despite the best efforts of the U.S. Army Corps of Engineers to control its flow through an elaborate system of dams and reservoirs. Scientists were full of prognostications and opinions.

A man in his seventies walked over. He wore jeans and cowboy boots and a long-sleeved Western shirt with fake pearl buttons. His gray hair was cut short, and his face was the color and texture of brown shoe leather. He sat down next to me and stared off into the late-morning sun. Finally, he took out some smoking tobacco and rolled himself a cigarette.

"Any good news?" he asked.

"Not much," I answered. "It looks like the farmers are in trouble. The reservoirs are drying up."

He nodded, then pulled some shards of tobacco from the end of his cigarette and wetted it with his lips.

"Damming a river is like stopping the blood in the veins," he said. "It's bound to cause trouble. 'Maybe it is the white man's gift to know how everything works,' a man once told me. It is our gift to know how everything fits together."

I make my way down to the thin ribbon of highway. A hand-painted sign greets me as I enter into Kyle: "Mommies and daddies. Please help us. Please. We want to be drug and alcohol free."

A group of teenage girls stands laughing and giggling in front of Little Wound School. They are like teenage girls everywhere, adjusting their makeup and fussing with their hair.

On the gravel apron of the Li'l Angel's convenience store three men lean against the bed of a pickup truck, smoking cigarettes and exchanging stories. They wave as I pass.

A solitary woman walks down the side of the highway carrying a plastic bag full of groceries. She does not look up but keeps up a steady stride in the direction of the sunset.

I continue out of town into the broad, rolling hills.

On the far edge of a field, a bison, the sacred *tatanka*, stands grazing at the base of a hill. He is as still and solid as a boulder.

A dog barks in the distance. The light cascades in silver shafts upon the hilltops.

There is a peace here that is difficult to express. It is not the peace of fatalism or despair or capitulation or indifference. It is the peace of belonging, of knowing you are of this land and from this land, that you stand on the shoulders of your ancestors who are present in every moment of your lives.

I continue toward the sunset.

Rough paths cut off into the hillsides. They lead to family compounds (*tiyospaye*)—extended family groups where the generations still live together and the children are raised as much by the aunts and uncles and grandmothers and grandfathers as they are by their parents. Sweat lodges huddle like small humps amidst the junk cars and children's bicycles by the sides of trailers. Huge cottonwood trees—the same kind that are cut down and carried to the Sun Dance ground to serve as the sacred center to which the dancers are tied—bend and rustle by the edge of dry creek beds.

I stop at the hill at Wounded Knee, where the bodies of 146 men, women, and children are buried in a mass grave. They were dragged here by local white civilians who were paid by the U.S. Army to clean up the killing field after the government soldiers massacred followers of Chief Big Foot's band at the creek across the road during the hard winter of 1890.*

*Sources vary on the number of dead and wounded, from 150 to more than 300. The reliable *Encyclopedia of the Great Plains* (Nebraska, 2004), edited by David J. Wishart, states 250–300.

A worn sign, recounting the historical events, sits at the base of the hill. A rutted clay path leads up to the graveyard. I make the climb, then step between the two crumbling brick pillars that mark the entrance to the burial area. Prayer ties flutter from the low, chain-link fence that surrounds the mass grave. Individual graves outside its perimeter are marked by wooden crosses and borders of small, white stones. They are covered with plastic flowers and figurines and teddy bears soggy from the rain.

In a corner plot rests the body of Zintkala Nuni, the Lost Bird, whose remains were repatriated here after living as a curiosity in white society. She had been found as an infant on the battlefield across the creek after the killings and was raised by one of the white soldiers to be a part of white American culture.

Like the priests and teachers who had taught the old man with the French fries, the soldier had thought he was performing an act of kindness. But the Lost Bird lived a sad and confused life, and she died lonely and isolated, far from her land and her people. She, too, was no longer herself. She, too, had lived her life as somebody else.

The setting sun glints off the words on the small obelisk that memorializes those buried in the mass grave: "Many innocent women and children who knew no wrong died here." The hills stretch off in peaceful rhythm toward the fiery glow of the sunset. The wind moves the prayer ties on the fence, and the bottoms of the gathering clouds burst forth in a symphony of oranges and magentas.

I bend down and place a small stone on the Lost Bird's grave. It is the least I can do to honor her memory.

Far off I hear the musical trill of the meadowlark, and I am filled with shame and wonder and an unfathomable sense of peace.

ORVILLE REDDEST'S
BOOT FENCE.

Tell Me About Your Story

Tell me about your story
Was there blood, sweat, or tears?
Maybe there was some glory
Over your last 100 years
Within your homeland
Prisoners they were
A powerful people
A powerful prayer
See the strength
Feel the pride
Run with nature
Nothing to hide

A little more heartache, it will never last
Strong in their ways, set in their path
Walking in beauty, all the way
Walking in beauty, the natives say
Brought them home, home to stay
This is our story
Of blood, sweat, and tears
No, there was no glory
But we will be here
The next 100 years

BY LAVELLE WARRIOR
10TH GRADE

A Journey Home

BY EMIL HER MANY HORSES
CURATOR IN THE OFFICE OF MUSEUM RESEARCH,
NATIONAL MUSEUM OF THE AMERICAN INDIAN

I grew up on the Rosebud Reservation because of my father's job, and we moved from Pine Ridge when I was very young. My seven siblings and I would attend the grade school in Rosebud. We lived on the Rosebud Reservation for so long that many people think that's where we are enrolled members. I have many great memories of both reservations. I didn't ride horses, but during the summertime I remember walking barefoot everyday, swimming at the dam at Rosebud, our local swimming hole, and eating wild chokecherries until my teeth were stained black or eating so many wild plums my stomach would hurt. As often as I could I tried to stay with my grandmother in Pine Ridge, where I played with my cousins. I would stay in Pine Ridge until the annual fair, where the Sun Dance was held in the morning, and in the afternoon and evening they held the powwow filled with competition dances. There were vendors with snow cones and cotton candy as well as carnival rides. I would return to Rosebud, where only a few weeks later they had their fair. Then it was time to go back to school. Surrounded by family, life as a child on the Rosebud and Pine Ridge Reservations seemed carefree and safe.

Life on the reservation is not as bleak as it sometimes appears. Our spiritual prayers, songs, and ceremonials have continued to survive. We are rich in our traditional culture. The Sun Dance continues to be a central ceremony, which is held around the summer solstice. This is a time when men and women bring their respective prayer request to a spiritual leader. To participate in the Sun Dance is a commitment which one does not take lightly. This is a commitment of prayer and living a good life not only for the betterment of one's self, but most importantly for the people.

The cottonwood tree that is placed in the middle of the Sun Dance circle helps the pledged dancers send their prayers to the *Wakan Tanka*, the Great Mystery. The base of the tree is covered with tobacco ties made of colored cloth and strung together with string. The tobacco ties are prayers offered to the *Wakan Tanka.* Also, attached to the tree are ropes representing pledges made by each individual male dancer. The pledge is one of personal sacrifice during the four-day dance in which one end of the rope is tied to the tree and the other end tied to two wooden pegs pierced in the chest of the dancer. Most pledges are made on behalf of sick relatives. After the dancers complete the four days of dancing, they dance out of the sacred circle in a single file. As the dancers exit the dance arena, family members and friends line up to thank the dancers. There are hugs, kisses, and handshakes extended to the dancers.

My family members danced at Fools Crow Sun Dance, which at the time was held at Porcupine, South Dakota, and I remember noticing that the elderly people giving a dancer's hand a two-handed handshake. They also told the dancers, "Thank You." I asked my dad, Leo, about the handshake and about the thank you. My dad said that the elderly people thank the dancers for dancing not only for their own individual reasons, but also for the people. There is a Lakota term that best explains this concept: "*Hecel lena oyate kin nipi kte*" ("That these people may live").

As I look back on my career as a museum curator at the Smithsonian's National Museum of the American Indian, I cannot help but think that the best preparation for my career was my experience of growing up on the Pine Ridge and Rosebud reservations in South Dakota. Although I am an enrolled member of the Oglala branch of the Lakota, which is located at Pine Ridge, I was raised on the Sicangu Lakota Reservation, located on the Rosebud Reservation. I consider both reservations as my home, even though I currently reside in Washington, D.C. For me "home" will always be where my immediate and extended family live.

EUGENE'S PIN CUSHION AND
ANUNKASAN (BALD EAGLE).

Crazy Horse

Crazy Horse
We hear what you say
One earth one mother
One does not sell the earth
The people walk upon
We are the land
How do we sell our mother
How do we sell the stars
How do we sell the air

Crazy Horse
We hear what you say
Too many people
Standing their ground
Standing the wrong ground
Predator's face he possessed a race
Possession a war that doesn't end
Children of god feed on children of earth
Days people don't care for people
These days are the hardest
Material fields material harvest
Decoration on chain that binds
Mirrors gold the people lose their minds

Crazy Horse
We hear what you say
One earth one mother
One does not sell the earth
The people walk upon
We are the land

Today is now and then
Dream smokes touch the clouds
On a day when death didn't die
Real world time tricks shadows lie
Red white perception deception
Predator tries civilizing us
But the tribes will not go without return
Genetic light from the other side
A song from the heart our hearts to give
The wild days the glory days live

Crazy Horse
We hear what you say
One earth one mother
One does not sell the earth
The people walk upon
We are the land
How do we sell our mother
How do we sell the stars
How do we sell the air

Crazy Horse
We hear what you say
Crazy Horse
We hear what you say
We are the seventh generation
We are the seventh generation

JOHN TRUDELL/ MADELINE SAHME, POETS

GRASS DANCER, ALLEN
COMMUNITY POWWOW.

BULL RIDING RODEO, SHARPS CORNER.

What If?

What if presidents never stole our homes?
What if they just left the Black Hills
Alone?
What if we weren't forced to live on
 a reservation?
Would we still have KILI station?
What if I didn't have to live as
 the white man wanted me to?
Does that mean I wouldn't have to
 copy everything they do?
What if our heritage was kept strong?
Would it be kept strong for long?
So I guess all I can ask is
"What if?" again and again
What if someone would listen?
What if?

STARR CUNY
9TH GRADE

LEROY MAKING
A *TIMPSILA* BRAID.

Spirit Lake

The Spirit Lake of the West, the place of the ancient ones,
I go there at dusk, the time when the day turns to night.
It is then that the ancestors come to sit on the banks
  and hold council.
I eagerly close my eyes and thank the great spirits for their wisdom.
They speak the words of all the generations of time.
They speak of the earth and all life
  and the way it was for thousands of years.
They speak of the sadness they feel
  for the way things have become.
Their wisdom holds the answers to making things better.
But no one listens, no one cares.
As I sit and listen to their voices
  and the ancient songs they sing.
I can feel their sadness and their pain at what they see.
I send up a prayer to the Creator that soon
  all will open their eyes and ears, that others
Will hear the wisdom of the ancient ones.
And that they will see the need for peace and change.
If you have a chance to visit "Spirit Lake" and the ancient ones,
  go there.
It is simple to find: just close your eyes and open your heart
  and your mind.
Ask the Grandfathers to take you there.
You will find it, for it is always waiting.
  We must listen and believe.

KRISTA RICHARD
10TH GRADE

Culture

I am fading away.
Slowly . . .
Day by day . . . .
I am so fragile now.
Anything more than a whisper
And I shall disappear.
I am forgotten in the hearts of man.
Young people don't care.
They don't understand.
I am buried down deep.
Stomped on . . . Forgotten . . . .
I am no longer respected,
Forever rejected . . . .
I am lost . . . . I am dying.
Do you know what I am saying
Or what I am implying?
Culture . . . . . .
Culture my friends is the key
So please don't reject or forget about me . . . .

ANGEL BIG CROW
9TH GRADE

ALLEN COMMUNITY HOUSING.

WATER TOWER, PINE RIDGE.

The Reservation Blues

if anyone feels that the rez does not fulfill your needs
well that right there is the reservation blues

these reservation blues can occur to anyone
these blues can consume elders and children very young
when I'm down it defines the reservation blues
then I go see my cousin who smokes, drinks, and chews
and I think about everyone who supports negative issues
I think about all the relationships, marriages, and divorces
and about all the money that supports Whiteclay's negative resources
I think about these issues and I stress 'em every day
but that's my rez for you and that's how it's going to stay

CASSIE PALMIER
10TH GRADE

THE SWIFT HAWK FAMILY
BURIES EARL SWIFT HAWK,
A WELL-RESPECTED MEDICINE MAN.

The Mists of Time

The older generations were very rich in memories of times past and as I write
I wish I listened more to their stories. Today, as I approach my own sunset,
I realize these few memories are history, even of this small area where I live.

The Lakota people are always struggling and will continue to do so. We are slowly
fading away with our language and culture, yet our place in history will leave
an impact in the future of the American people.

Ho Hecetu Welo
(That's All Right Now).

QUINCY RED FEATHER, ELDER

In the End

I lay in my room and stare into space
hoping everything would fall into place.
My life's been so crazy,
Even I wonder why.
Everything seems perfect,
But nothing seems right.
It feels like a set up.
I feel I've been robbed
of special moments and memories,
but most of all a father's love.
But what can I do?
What more can I say?
Except life has lots of tricks
that get thrown your way.
You just have to deal with them
The best you can.
And even though its hard to do
I believe everything happens for a reason.
And life goes on,
But I wish he was here,
every day of every year.
Sometimes I get lost in my thoughts
and for a split second I think he's still here.
Then reality comes crashing down,
followed by my tears.
I don't even remember him,
but that makes me miss him more.
I know what you're thinking.
How could you miss somebody that you don't even know?

All I can say is
it's a yearning in my heart that only seems to grow.
And it gets stronger all the time,
every time I close my eyes
and remember him in memories,
memories that aren't even mine.
I could sit and think for hours
about everything that could have been,
everything we could have had
all cut short in an instant.
Sometimes I wish it was all a bad dream,
but I have to settle for reality.
In the end all I can do
is wish and dream and end up settling for reality.

DENA LONE HILL
10TH GRADE

DAYBREAK.

The Ceremony Acknowledging the 175th Anniversary of the Establishment of the Bureau of Indian Affairs

(8 September 2000)

BY KEVIN GOVER
DIRECTOR, NATIONAL MUSEUM
OF THE AMERICAN INDIAN*

In March of 1824, President James Monroe established the Office of Indian Affairs in the Department of War. Its mission was to conduct the nation's business with regard to Indian affairs. We have come together today to mark the first 175 years of the institution now known as the Bureau of Indian Affairs.

It is appropriate that we do so in the first year of a new century and a new millennium, a time when our leaders are reflecting on what lies ahead and preparing for those challenges. Before looking ahead, though, this institution must first look back and reflect on what it has wrought and, by doing so, come to know that this is no occasion for celebration; rather it is time for reflection and contemplation, a time for sorrowful truths to be spoken, a time for contrition.

We must first reconcile ourselves to the fact that the works of this agency have at various times profoundly harmed the communities it was meant to serve. From the very beginning, the Office of Indian Affairs was an instrument by which the United States enforced its ambition against the Indian nations and Indian people who stood in its path. And, so, the first mission of this institution was to execute the removal of the Southeastern tribal nations. By threat, deceit, and force, these great tribal nations were made to march 1,000 miles to the west, leaving thousands of their old, their young, and their infirm in hasty graves along the Trail of Tears. As the nation looked to the West for more land, this agency participated in the ethnic cleansing that befell the Western tribes. War necessarily begets tragedy; the war for the West was no exception. Yet, in these more enlightened times, it must be acknowledged that the deliberate spread of disease, the decimation of the mighty bison herds, the use of the poison alcohol to destroy mind and body, and the cowardly killing of women and children made for tragedy on a scale so ghastly that it cannot be dismissed as merely the inevitable consequence of the clash of competing ways of life.

This agency and the good people in it failed in the mission to prevent the devastation. And so great nations of patriot warriors fell. We will never push aside the memory of unnecessary and violent death at places such as Sand Creek, the banks of the Washita River, and Wounded Knee.

Nor did the consequences of war have to include the futile and destructive efforts to annihilate Indian cultures. After the devastation of tribal economies and the deliberate creation of tribal dependence on the services provided by this agency, this agency set out to destroy all things Indian.

*At the time Kevin Gover gave this address he was Assistant Secretary of Indian Affairs in the U.S. Department of the Interior.

This agency forbade the speaking of Indian languages, prohibited the conduct of traditional religious activities, outlawed traditional government, and made Indian people ashamed of who they were. Worst of all, the Bureau of Indian Affairs (BIA) committed these acts against the children entrusted to its boarding schools, brutalizing them emotionally, psychologically, physically, and spiritually. Even in this era of self-determination, when the BIA is at long last serving as an advocate for Indian people in an atmosphere of mutual respect, the legacy of these misdeeds haunts us. The trauma of shame, fear, and anger has passed from one generation to the next and manifests itself in the rampant alcoholism, drug abuse, and domestic violence that plague Indian country. Many of our people live lives of unrelenting tragedy as Indian families suffer the ruin of lives by alcoholism, suicides made of shame and despair, and violent death at the hands of one another. So many of the maladies suffered today in Indian country result from the failures of this agency. Poverty, ignorance, and disease have been the products of this agency's work.

And so, today, I stand before you as the leader of an institution that, in the past, has committed acts so terrible that they infect, diminish, and destroy the lives of Indian people decades later, generations later. These things occurred despite the efforts of many good people with good hearts who sought to prevent them. These wrongs must be acknowledged, if the healing is to begin.

I do not speak today for the United States. That is the province of the nation's elected leaders, and I would not presume to speak on their behalf. I am empowered, however, to speak on behalf of this agency, the Bureau of

THE MASS GRAVESITE
AT WOUNDED KNEE.

Indian Affairs, and I am quite certain that the words that follow reflect the hearts of its 10,000 employees.

Let us begin by expressing our profound sorrow for what this agency has done in the past. Just like you, when we think of these misdeeds and their tragic consequences, our hearts break, and our grief is as pure and complete as yours. We desperately wish that we could change this history, but, of course, we cannot. On behalf of the Bureau of Indian Affairs, I extend this formal apology to Indian people for the historical conduct of this agency.

And while the BIA employees of today did not commit these wrongs, we acknowledge that the institution we serve did. We accept this inheritance, this legacy of racism and inhumanity. And, by accepting this legacy, we accept also the moral responsibility of putting things right.

We, therefore, begin this important work anew and make a new commitment to the people and communities that we serve, a commitment born of the dedication we share with you to the cause of renewed hope and prosperity for Indian country. Never again will this agency stand silent when hate and violence are committed against Indians. Never again will we allow policy to proceed from the assumption that Indians possess less human genius than the other races. Never again will we be complicit in the theft of Indian property. Never again will we appoint false leaders who serve purposes other than those of the tribes. Never again will we allow unflattering and stereotypical images of Indian people to deface the halls of government or lead the American people to shallow and ignorant beliefs about Indians. Never again will we attack your religions, your languages, your rituals, or any of your tribal ways. Never again will we seize your children, nor teach them to be ashamed of who they are. Never again.

We cannot yet ask your forgiveness, not while the burdens of this agency's history weigh so heavily on tribal communities. What we do ask is that, together, we allow the healing to begin: As you return to your homes, and as you talk with your people, please tell them that the time of dying is at its end. Tell your children that the time of shame and fear is over. Tell your young men and women to replace their anger with hope and love for their people. Together we must wipe the tears of seven generations. Together we must allow our broken hearts to mend. Together we will face a challenging world with confidence and trust. Together let us resolve that, when our future leaders gather to discuss the history of this institution, it will be time to celebrate the rebirth of joy, freedom, and progress for the Indian nations. The Bureau of Indian Affairs was born in 1824 in a time of war on Indian people. May it live in the year 2000 and beyond as an instrument of their prosperity.

Source: *http://www.twofrog.com/gover.html.*

NEVILLE AND HIS
GRANDDAUGHTER.

Ledger Drawings by Dwayne Wilcox

Dwayne Wilcox was born and raised on the Pine Ridge Reservation and is an enrolled member of the Oglala Lakota people. He has lived and worked in Rapid City, South Dakota, for many years. His artwork has won numerous awards, including First Place in Mixed Media and Best of Division at the Heard Museum Indian Art Market in 2013 and 2008 and First Place in Ledger Art at the Santa Fe Indian Art Market in 2013 and 2007. His artwork has also been commissioned and exhibited by museums throughout the United States, including the Charles M. Russell Museum in Great Falls, Montana, Hood Museum of Art at Dartmouth College, Peabody Essex Museum in Salem, Massachusetts, Philbrook Museum in Tulsa, Oklahoma, Portland (OR) Art Museum, San Diego Museum of Art, and Smithsonian National Museum of the American Indian in New York City. His Website is *www.dwaynewilcox@rushmore.com*.

About My Work

"I have been drawing all my life but, in 1988, committed myself to doing what I was put on this road for: recovery and enlightenment. So I worked very hard to find and research ledger drawings wherever I could find them, including the Smithsonian Institution and other museums that collect ledger drawings. To the many friends who were helpful in this pursuit, thank you. I find that my friends and family influence my work by the way they communicate and tell a joke or a story. This is what I see as everyday life."

Why Humor?

"In the Lakota way, humor is medicine and helps us heal. That is why there is the Sacred Clown. My drawings are meant to reflect that kind of humor and the traditional life-ways."

Why Lined Paper?

"Pictographs, our traditional visual language, were once put on familiar things such as hides. That changed with the disappearance of the bison and the loss of freedom to hunt, when the reservations bound the native people. The first paper on the Great Plains was found in used ledger books from white merchants. That paper became a new medium to my people, in addition to the colored pencils and inks available for trade. Like beads and beadwork, which were also traded, paper from ledgers has become a traditional form of art called ledger art."

CHEYENNES RUN

FT. ROBINSON.

ACRYLIC ON 1897 LEDGER PAPER:

14" x 8.5" (2001).

WOW, REAL FULL-BLOODED WHITE PEOPLE.
INK AND COLORED PENCIL ON 1893 LEDGER PAPER:
17.5" x 11.5" (2008).

CHEESE WITH THAT WHINE.
INK AND COLORED PENCIL
ON 1882 LEDGER PAPER:
15.25" x 10.75" (2007).

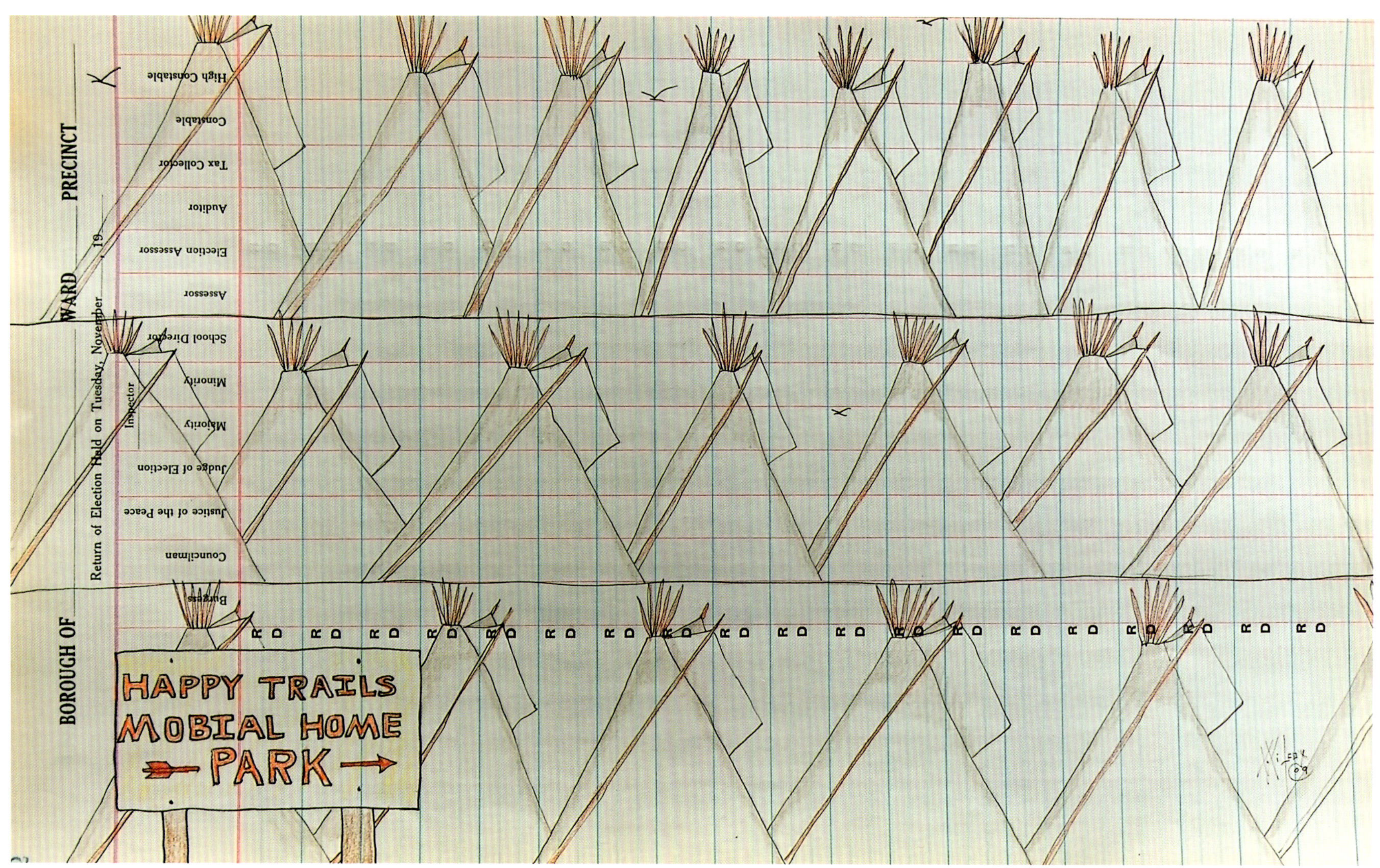

FIRST MOBILE HOMES.
INK AND COLORED PENCIL
ON 1936 LEDGER PAPER:
17" x 11" (2009).

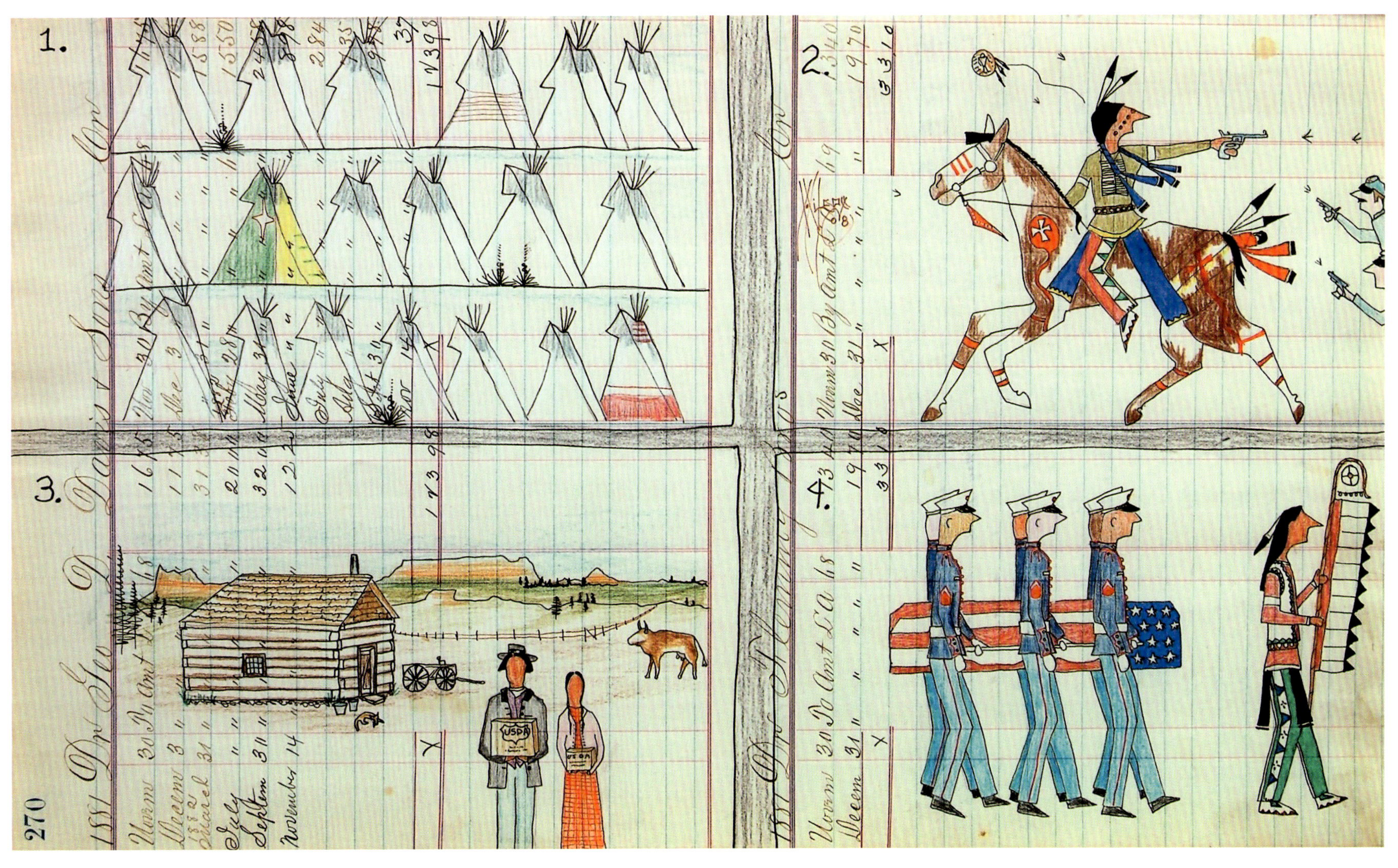

FROM HERE TO ETERNITY.
INK AND COLORED PENCIL
ON 1881 LEDGER PAPER:
15.25" x 10.75" (2008).

HANG IN THERE BABY.
INK AND COLORED PENCIL
ON 1893 LEDGER PAPER:
17.5" x 11.5" (2005).

WASH DAY.
INK AND COLORED PENCIL
ON 1893 LEDGER PAPER:
17.5" x 11.5" (2006).

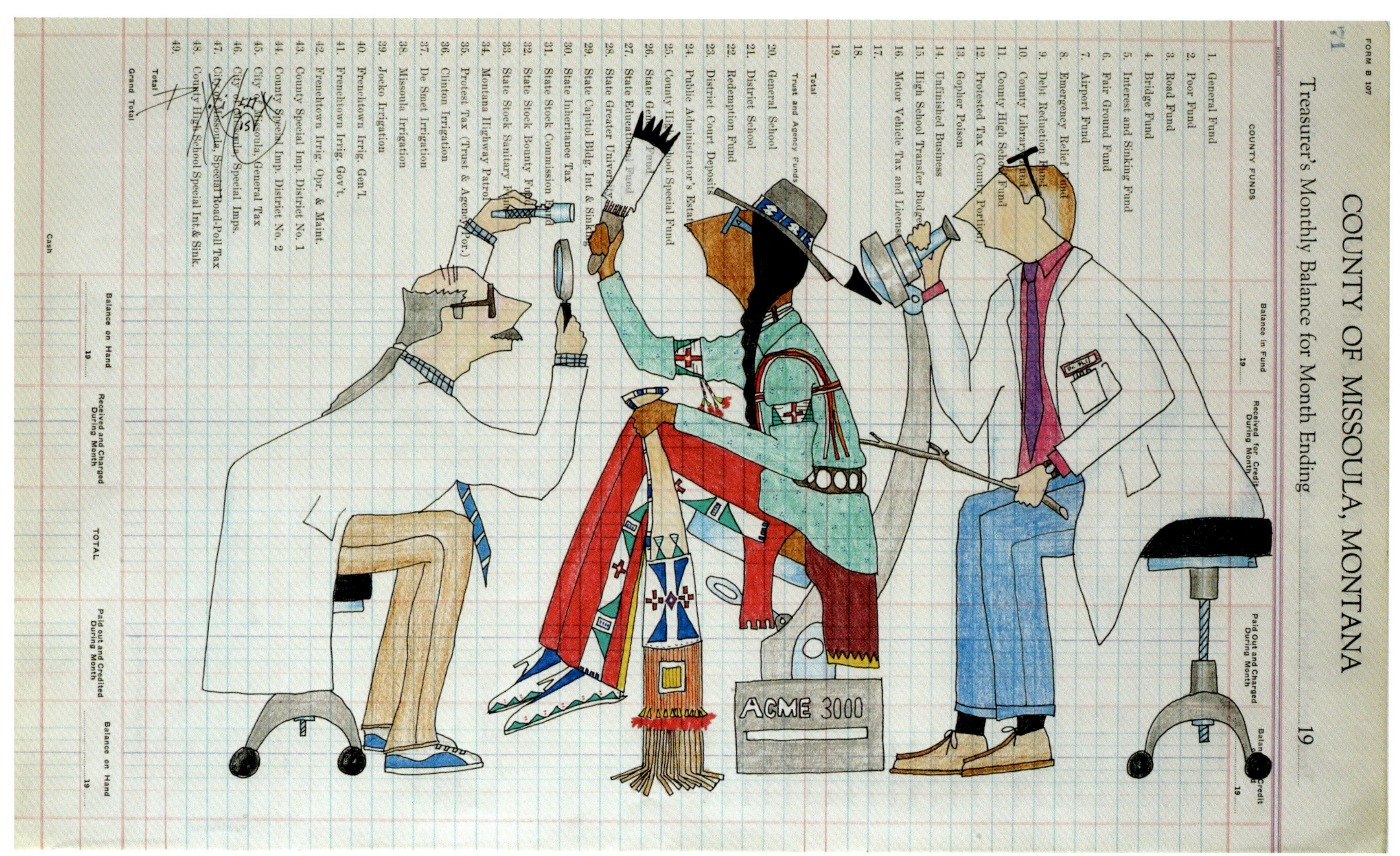

DEPARTMENT OF INDIGENOUS STUDIES.
INK AND COLORED PENCIL ON
CIRCA 1900 LEDGER PAPER:
14.25" X 8.75" (2015).

Reddest Family Album

The following images (on pages 131–58) are from the archives of the Reddest Family of Lost Dog Creek, except for two images of Spotted Horse, which were given to me by his relatives, Marian and Chubb White Mouse. Most of the images belonged to Thomas Hollow Head and were of his various family members. Ellen Hollow Head, daughter of Thomas, married Eugene Reddest (Comes Out First) from the Rosebud Reservation, to the east of the Pine Ridge Reservation. Eugene moved to Lost Dog Creek, where he and Ellen raised their family. The family archive was left to Ellen when Thomas passed away.

The traditional way of life had been for families to travel and camp in various places throughout the year. The U.S. government gave parcels to Lakota people in order to have them settle down in one spot on reservation land. The hope was that the Lakota, by owning their own land and assuming the life of a farmer, would become less tribal and assimilate more easily into white society.

Thomas was given a parcel of 360 acres near Potato Creek that he named Lost Dog Creek. He was also given some furniture and Holstein cows. When Ellen Hollow Head turned eighteen, she, too, was given furniture, as was the government policy at the time. Today, this no longer happens, and family members trying to start a home look for furniture at second-hand stores and yard sales.

Eugene Reddest owned land on the Rosebud Reservation and Standing Rock Reservation. When he passed on, he left his daughter, Andrea, the land on Standing Rock in North Dakota. The tribe leases her land to ranchers for grazing or growing hay. The small parcel brings her an annual income of $63.

Eugene and Ellen's children were born and raised at Lost Dog Creek, where they stayed home most of the time, spoke only Lakota, and would hide down by the creek when strangers came to visit. They spent their time there on the property with extended family. There, they learned the traditional Lakota ways and how to homestead, including hunting, gathering, gardening, horseback riding, animal husbandry, finding and using medicinal plants, and more. Happily, they continued this lifestyle until the U.S. government instituted the policy of forcing native children to attend boarding schools, where the goal was to teach values and skills needed to assimilate into the dominant white society. In these boarding schools, they were kept from speaking any language other than English, were made to dress like Caucasians and attend Christian churches, performed manual labor jobs, and were not allowed to participate in any traditional rituals or to cherish things representing their native culture. The children at these schools were brought from various reservations and indigenous tribes in order to help dilute their native cultures.

This policy of forced education in the boarding schools lasted until the mid-twentieth century and affected all the family's children for two generations. Andrea Marshall, daughter of Eugene and Ellen, was sent to a boarding school in Rosebud. Later, she was moved to Holy Rosary Mission School in Pine Ridge. There, she was treated so poorly that she repeatedly ran away with friends and walked home. The law required her family to return her to the boarding school or the parents could be taken to jail. In reflection, when a few non-native friends and I were sitting around discussing the appreciation we shared for our college experience, Eugene's son, Duane, who is our age, commented in disbelief that the boarding schools had been such a horrible experience that the thought of anyone choosing to continue with school by their own choice had never even entered his mind.

To this day, Reddest Family members live at Lost Dog Creek, where they raise their families and carry on many of the Lakota traditions amidst a changing world. Those young enough to attend school are picked up by bus to attend schools an hour's drive away. Those who are lucky enough to find jobs amidst the extremely high unemployment rate on the reservation commute up to an hour and a half each way. Their home is still a very beautiful place, and they are welcoming to friends of their various relations. It is there where my introduction to Lakota people and their way of life began in 1992, and, my understanding of that life continues to grow with each visit.

A GOLDEN EAGLE PLUME AND PORCUPINE MEDICINE WHEEL MADE FOR CHARLYN BULL BEAR'S NAMING CEREMONY, IN WHICH SHE INHERITED HER GRANDMOTHER ANDREA REDDEST MARSHALL'S INDIAN NAME, *WAPHI AGLI WEIN* (BRINGS HOME THE FLAG), 2004.

A PHOTOGRAPH OF THOMAS HOLLOW HEAD'S UNCLE IN A PORCUPINE QUILL FRAME MADE BY ELLEN HOLLOW HEAD, CIRCA 1865.

JOBSON HOLLOW HEAD AND SISTER, SIBLINGS OF THOMAS HOLLOW HEAD, CIRCA 1890. MOST OF THE OLDER IMAGES IN THE FAMILY ARCHIVE CAME FROM THE FAMILY OF THOMAS HOLLOW HEAD. WHEN HE PASSED ON TO THE OTHER SIDE, ELLEN HOLLOW HEAD, EUGENE REDDEST'S WIFE, INHERITED THEM.

NEWSPAPER CUTOUT, DATE UNKNOWN. THE NAMES OF THE CHIEFS WERE WRITTEN BY EUGENE REDDEST.

BUFFALO BILL CODY'S *WILD WEST SHOW*, INCLUDING RELATIVES OF THOMAS HOLLOW HEAD, CIRCA 1883–1893.

A PORTRAIT OF TWO BOYS,
CIRCA 1880.

A *CARTE DE VISITE* CABINET CARD PORTRAIT OF AN UNIDENTIFIED WOMAN, CIRCA 1890.

(LEFT) AN UNIDENTIFIED WOMAN, CIRCA 1880.
(RIGHT) GOOD VOICE, A SURVIVOR OF THE BATTLE OF THE LITTLE BIG HORN, CIRCA 1880.

(LEFT) THREE GENERATIONS OF THE RED CLOUD FAMILY, BY J. A. MILLER, GORDON, NEBRASKA, 1909.
(RIGHT) A STUDIO PORTRAIT OF AN UNIDENTIFIED WOMAN, CIRCA 1910.

SPOTTED HORSE, CIRCA 1890, A RELATION AND MEDICINE MAN WHO IS SAID TO BE A SURVIVOR OF THE BATTLE OF THE LITTLE BIG HORN.

SPOTTED HORSE'S SON,
CIRCA 1940.

TRADITIONAL DANCE
REGALIA FOR A POWWOW,
CIRCA 1890.

A DRUM GROUP AT A POWWOW, CIRCA 1920. IN THE OLD DAYS, POWWOWS WERE OFTEN OUTSIDE WITHOUT EVEN A SHADE ARBOR.

TWO HIGH BULL BROTHERS ON THE LEFT AND EUGENE REDDEST ON THE RIGHT IN TRADITIONAL POWWOW DANCE OUTFITS, CIRCA 1947.

POWWOW DANCING ON
THE PINE RIDGE RESERVA-
TION, CIRCA 1920.THIS IMAGE
SHOWS A HEYOKAH DANCER
IN LONG UNDERWEAR,
FULFILLING A DREAM IN
THE DANCE.

GRANDMOTHER SARAH
HOLLOW HEAD (IN THE
STRIPED SHAWL), CIRCA 1942.

RAYMOND CUTT AND HIS FAMILY, CIRCA 1950. RAYMOND WAS A MEDICINE MAN FROM WANBLEE, SOUTH DAKOTA, WHOSE CEREMONIES ANDREA REDDEST MARSHALL AND HER FAMILY WOULD FREQUENTLY ATTEND.

(LEFT) ERNEST BLUE LEGS, ORVILLE REDDEST, AND BESSIE WHITE (ANDREA'S GRAND-MOTHER), CIRCA 1940.
(RIGHT) MOSES BULL MAN, CIRCA 1940.

(LEFT) ANNIE HOLLOW HEAD AND MOSES BULL MAN, CIRCA 1945. SOON AFTER HE RETURNED FROM WORLD WAR II, HE PASSED AWAY AS A RESULT OF COMPLICATIONS FROM BEING SHOT IN THE STOMACH WHILE IN THE SOUTH PACIFIC. (RIGHT) UNCLE ERNEST BLUE LEGS, WHO RETURNED FROM WORLD WAR II WITH A JAPANESE FLAG IN HIS POSSESSION AND GAVE THE FLAG AND AN INDIAN NAME (*WAPHI AGLI WEIN*, OR BRINGS HOME THE FLAG) TO ANDREA, CIRCA 1945.

A DINNER, CIRCA 1945, HONORING ERNEST BLUE LEGS AFTER HIS SAFE RETURN FROM SERVING IN THE SOUTH PACIFIC DURING WORLD WAR II.

A POTATO CREEK POWWOW,
CIRCA 1945, IN CELEBRATION
OF ERNEST BLUE LEGS'S SAFE
RETURN FROM WORLD WAR II.

(LEFT) ORVILLE REDDEST (AS A BOY) AND MOSES BULL MAN, CIRCA 1946. (RIGHT) ORVILLE REDDEST AND ANDREA REDDEST (WHOSE MARRIED NAME BECAME MARSHALL), CIRCA 1946.

ERNEST BLUE LEGS AT LOST DOG CREEK, CIRCA 1947. HE WAS VERY POPULAR AFTER RETURNING FROM MILITARY SERVICE IN WORLD WAR II.

THOMAS HOLLOW HEAD (#2)
AND HIS BROTHERS,
CIRCA 1915.

MEN WHO WERE BUILDING SAINT TIMOTHY EPISCOPAL CHURCH IN POTATO CREEK, CIRCA 1950. YEARS LATER, ORVILLE REDDEST WOULD PREACH SERMONS HERE.

(LEFT) ELLEN HOLLOW HEAD (WHO MARRIED EUGENE REDDEST), CIRCA 1940. (RIGHT) ERNEST BLUE LEGS (TOP LEFT), CHARLIE RED HORSE (TOP RIGHT), AND THEIR THREE SISTERS (LEFT TO RIGHT: ELLEN, SARAH, AND MARTHA HOLLOW HEAD) HAULING WATER, CIRCA 1940.

(LEFT TO RIGHT) ERNEST BLUE LEGS (WHO WAS TAKEN IN, OR ADOPTED BY, BESSIE WHITE), BESSIE WHITE (EMMA HOLLOW HEAD'S SISTER WHO WAS CONSIDERED A GRANDMOTHER TO THE REDDEST CHILDREN), AND AN UNIDENTIFIED WOMAN, CIRCA 1940.

Prairie Wind

Everyday

Blows in my hair

Messing it up a bit

I laugh as I think

Not again

KRISTIN BRINGS PLENTY
11TH GRADE

ANDREA REDDEST MARSHALL
IN FRONT OF HER GRAND-
PARENTS' CABIN, CIRCA 1958.

Artist's Statement

During the summer of 1992, I was given the opportunity to join a friend and visit Lost Dog Creek, the family compound of the Reddest Family on the Pine Ridge Reservation in southwestern South Dakota. There, I was introduced to Eugene Reddest, the elder of the family and a man I viewed as a holy man. "Grandfather Eugene," as many called him, welcomed me into his home, where for the next month we worked together and shared stories and life experiences. Eventually, he invited me to attend an *inipi* (a sacred sweat-lodge ceremony for cleansing and prayer) and witness *humbeleche* (vision quests). I did so then and on future trips participated in and observed many Lakota rituals, including Sun Dances and naming (*yuwipis*) and give-away (*wopila*) ceremonies.

While visiting the Reddest family and bearing witness to their lives, I began to see the reservation as a magnificent place to be, where I could learn about life and share life's lessons. As a photographer, I also recognized it as a source of material for visual commentary, but I was aware of the hostility of my hosts to any real (or imagined) deprecation of their rituals. From that very first *inipi* ceremony, I have been moved by the prayer ceremony and everyone sitting on the earth in the darkened, womb-shaped shelter that surrounds a pit, where red-hot rocks are placed and water is poured over them, creating a hot steam bath that is physically challenging and inspirational. Throughout, Lakota prayer songs are sung while cleansing steam engulfs one's complete being. Lodges can be very difficult or easy, but they are always rejuvenating.

I have always used the photographic process as a tool for exploring the world around me. It has been especially important for me, as a photographer, to be considerate of and sensitive to the Lakota attitude toward tribal rituals. As history tells us, photography played a large role in contributing to the U.S. government outlawing all traditional Lakota spiritual practices and rituals for some forty years during the late-nineteenth and early-twentieth centuries. Photography and other tools of documentarians were used to convince the U.S. government that the native people were practicing barbaric rituals. Taken out of context, the government outlawed all religious practices, even the *inipi* ceremony. For those forty years, traditional Lakota practices were kept alive by those who were willing to risk imprisonment by secretly having their ceremonies while hiding in the plains. Today, the religious practices are again legal and growing in popularity, but the distrust of photography and documentarians still exists and understandably so.

Eugene was a pipe carrier (the keeper of the *c'anupa*, the sacred peace pipe) who followed the traditional Lakota spiritual path. For good reason, many Lakota on this path would not want to share the traditions with outsiders. But Eugene welcomed others, regardless of their background, if he believed they were sincere, with a heartfelt intention to be present with an open mind. He accepted non-natives by keeping the medicine wheel in mind with the four directional colors, each color, according to Black Elk, representing the races of humanity coming together in the Sacred Hoop: red (north), yellow (east), white (south), and black (west).

Eugene and his cousin, Tommy Crow, are among the most humble and inspirational teachers I have ever met. Regretfully, both have passed on, as they once said, "to be with relations on the other side." They taught through their actions with the best intentions and a great sense of humor. They had so little materialistically yet gave so much. I remember, during my first extended visit, that I wanted to give Eugene a special gift to thank him for his hospitality. I thought long and hard to find something he could really use and would appreciate. I settled on a special fossilized turtle token for his altar. He was very grateful for the gift and seemed honored to receive it. On my next visit, I looked around to see this gift in a visible place of honor. It was nowhere to be seen in his modest home. I asked him about its whereabouts. He responded by saying he liked it so much that he chose to give it away. He wanted others to have the pleasure of receiving it as a gift, too.

This generosity is a reflection of the Lakota philosophy of *wawókiye*, meaning to help another with no expectation of reward or payment, as exemplified in the *wopila* (or give-away) ceremony. In the world I grew up in, back in New England, the norm for most rituals and celebrations—funerals, graduations, honorings, memorials, religious initiation ceremonies, weddings, and many others—is for the person or people being honored to receive gifts and support from those attending. The Lakota, however, traditionally do the opposite: In Lakota culture, a family celebrating an important event honors the people attending with a *wopila* (gift), where visitors are fed and all are given gifts. To see this practice in a place such as the Pine Ridge Reservation, where the unemployment rate is among the nation's highest and poverty is extreme, is awe-inspiring. Families will spend up to a year making gifts as grand as Lone Star quilts, saving what little money they can give in abundance and splendor in order to show appreciation and honor those who come to share respect for the ceremony's honoree. Generosity is considered a true Lakota virtue.

The first time I witnessed this practice was at a memorial dinner for Eugene's wife, Ellen Hollow Head, who had died a year earlier. We prepared food for days. Gifts had been made and gathered by the extended family during that year. The memorial was held at a local powwow

EUGENE LAUGHING BY THE *INIPI* (SWEAT LODGE). USED BY PERMISSION.

grounds under a shade arbor made of pine boughs used for community celebrations. The service was announced over the reservation's community radio station (KILI, "The Voice of the Lakota Nation," at 90.1 FM) in order to spread the word. Anyone, whether they knew Ellen or not, was invited to come out of respect for the family and their loss.

More than 200 people attended. Food was plentiful for all; in fact, everyone had more than they could possibly eat. I commented to a friend that there was so much food we would probably be taking home a ton of leftovers. She smiled and said we would stay there until the food was gone. I looked over at the tables full of food and was sure we would be there for days. She then said we should just keep going around and serving food. As we continued to serve the food, people began pulling out all sorts of containers and filling them. Families left with grocery bags full of food, carrying them home to share with an even wider circle.

I have returned to the reservation at least once every year since 1992, and my connection to the people has grown with each trip. Over the years, my photographing has become acceptable in a wide variety of daily situations, and people of the reservation seem genuinely to appreciate my photos, which have been circulated widely among the tribe. On each subsequent visit, I have been invited to photograph a larger panorama of the life of the tribe. It is important, I believe, that a record be made to chronicle the real life of the modern Lakota, one that neither highlights nor avoids the fact that these still-proud people have become an abjectly poor nation.

The reality of the poverty cannot be denied. The Pine Ridge Reservation was the poorest county in the United States for fifty years running; only recently has another county, also a reservation in South Dakota, surpassed it in economic hardship. The harsh reality of reservation life is comparable with life in the Third World.

Prior to visiting a reservation, I had seen extreme poverty in Central America and was shocked by the harsh conditions people had to endure so close to the borders of the United States. But, at Pine Ridge, I realized the depths of poverty existing within the United States. The poverty of the Pine Ridge and other reservations was shocking to me at the time and continues to shock me these many years later. The statistics can overwhelm both head and heart. Sixty-nine percent of children on the reservation live in poverty. People still freeze to death in their own homes during winter, and the number of unemployed adults fluctuates between eighty-five and (in a good year) fifty-five percent. Many Lakota do not have running water, only hand pumps and outhouses. According to a publication by the Red Cloud Indian School, on Pine Ridge Reservation today there are approximately

36,000 Lakota people, half of whom who are under the age of eighteen. Gangs are a problem. The per-capita income average in 2018 was $7,773; in 2010, it was around $4,000. Life expectancy of Lakota males is now forty-seven compared to fifty-five in 2010, and for females it is fifty-two compared to sixty in 2010. Compare those figures with the U.S. average, which has remained steady at seventy-six for males and eighty-one for females. The infant mortality rate is twice the national average, and the suicide rate is seventy-two percent higher than the national rate. Thirty-seven percent of the population is diabetic. Alcoholism is a major problem, partially due to such high unemployment rates. While Pine Ridge has elected to be a "dry county," some 4,000,000 cans and bottles of beer were sold a year—that's nearly 11,000 a day—just two miles south of the reservation in Whiteclay, Nebraska, whose official population is twenty-two. That pipeline to alcohol changed on September 29, 2017, when the Nebraska Supreme Court shut down the sale of beer there. With statistics such as these, how or why would one choose to ignore the poverty when speaking of reservation life?

COVER TO "REMEMBER ME," ELLEN HOLLOW HEAD'S LAKOTA AND ENGLISH HYMNAL, WHICH SHE MADE AT AGE SIXTEEN (IN 1930) AND DECORATED WITH PORCUPINE QUILLS.

About fifteen years ago, I saw the film *Rabbit Proof Fence* (2002), about Australia's sanctioned treatment of its aboriginal people. The film is a beautifully made portrayal of the Australian government's policy of removing indigenous children from their parents against their will and sending them off to boarding schools, where they would be forced to assimilate into the white society, leaving behind their traditional languages and culture. The film's closing credits acknowledged that the Australian government implemented this harsh practice well into the 1970s.

I can still recall the rumbles of horror I heard from the audience, disbelief that the Australians would back such inhumane treatment of their own first citizens and, worse, so recently in history. What this American film audience and others throughout the nation clearly did not realize was that the United States also enforced a similar policy, from the late-nineteenth century into the 1960s and 70s. Many Lakota friends my age can share firsthand experiences of being physically abused and punished for things as slight as asking where the outhouse is in Lakota, because they had not yet learned the words in English. I mention this story here because it so clearly exemplifies the tendency of outsiders to look at difficulties people endure and view them as being in the past or out of reach. The need to be reminded of such realities, to consider similar contemporary situations, and to avoid complacency is partial inspiration for my putting this book together, now presented in an updated and expanded edition.

How and why can things be so unfair and unjust? In terms of wealth, as I grew up considering it, these people are living amongst extreme poverty, yet they strike me as a people with so much to teach the dominant society. I also recognize the wealth the Lakota possess. While the predominant white culture views wealth as the gathering of materialistic possessions, the Lakota do not. As a Lakota friend once told me, "Whatever you have and cherish most, give it away. That way it will bring good things to others, and more good things will come your way."

My experience on the reservation verifies that living within their traditional values is also a valuable form of wealth, even though it does not eradicate the need for better living conditions. Their economic poverty reminds me to place my materialistic desires in check, to remember just how much opportunity I have relative to much of the world.

Alma Richards, another dear Lakota friend, spoke to me of Lakota commandments or virtues that she lived by. In *Lakota Commandments* (on page 20), she mentions thirteen; among the most common are bravery, fortitude, generosity, humility, and wisdom, which are described well in *The Sioux* (1964) by Royal B. Hasserick and *The Lakota Way: Stories and Lessons for Living* (2001) by Joseph M. Marshall, III. Bravery is viewed as living with courage, as having a strong heart and keeping honor in mind. Fortitude is the willingness and ability to endure physical hardship for the good of oneself or others. As Hasserick and Marshall point out, one gains good fortune in Lakota culture by being generous, by helping those in need. Thus, rather than being a burden to society, the indigent become a necessary vehicle for the successful to gain social status. Wisdom, as it is considered, is not attained solely through intelligence but includes the ability to advise, arbitrate disputes, give counsel, inspire and lead, and get along with others.

When I was first invited to attend a Lakota Sun Dance ceremony—where the prayer ritual involves physical sacrifice for males, including the piercing of pectoral muscles before being tied to the Sun Dance cottonwood tree so that the self through the flesh might be torn away—I felt I should attend primarily to respect and support my host community. To my surprise, the ceremony I witnessed affected me in ways I never could have foreseen. My preconceived notion was of a ceremony over the edge, in which the degree of sacrifice is unnecessary and extreme could not have been more wrong. What I found was one of the most beautiful and memorable services I have ever witnessed.

Drumming and singing are integral parts of a Sun Dance. It is a powerful force that brings forth strength and energy, a connection between the dancers, supporters, and *Tunkasila* (the Great Spirit). During the four-day ceremony, while the dancers dance to the Sun Dance tree in the center circle, supporters come and stand under a circular shade arbor. Throughout the ceremony one dancer, in particular, keeps his focus on the eyes of a single supporter and vice versa. Their gaze towards each other has a continuous intensity I had never seen between two individuals. I was so moved by it I asked around until someone told me about the two. I learned they were father and son. The son was dancing as a commitment to assist his father, who had been diagnosed with terminal cancer. The father had been told he had terminal cancer, that nothing could be done, and that he would die within a month or two at most. The son followed the traditional ways and committed to the Sun Dance for four consecutive years as a sacrifice to assist his father.

Traditional Lakota rituals are done in a cycle of four years. Once one begins the commitment, he or she will complete the cycle to help the people. Realizing the son was making this very difficult sacrifice for his father was truly humbling. He could not know whether his prayers would be answered or if his sacrifice would help his father live. But no one could doubt that the act of commitment created one of the most tightly connected bonds between a father and son. For the son to show his father how much he cared, and for the father to be there supporting him in honor and acceptance of his sacrifice, is comparable to the sacrifice a woman makes to bring a child into the world. I have been told that honoring the sacrifice a mother gives in childbirth is where the meaning of the Sun Dance comes from.

Rather than feeling that the Sun Dance ritual was too extreme, as I previously believed, I left in wonder, for I had just witnessed one of the most sincerely moving and meaningful actions I would ever see not only between individual participants of the ritual, but the people as a whole. Since that time, I have witnessed many equally moving circumstances of support in the Lakota world between mothers and daughters, grandparents and grandchildren, and supportive friends.

Creating a book I can be proud of about the Oglala Lakota living on the Pine Ridge Reservation is a huge challenge. Attempting to create one that my Lakota friends will feel is worthy is even more daunting. I find myself thinking of the many times I have sat with Lakota people during rituals and been told how they do things: "This is the way it is done, the way it is always done and has always been done." I have listened and accepted the sincerity in their voices. Yet when I participate at a similar ritual elsewhere and am told it is the same, the procedure is not exactly the same. At first this incongruity seemed difficult to accept. But, emerging from a culture

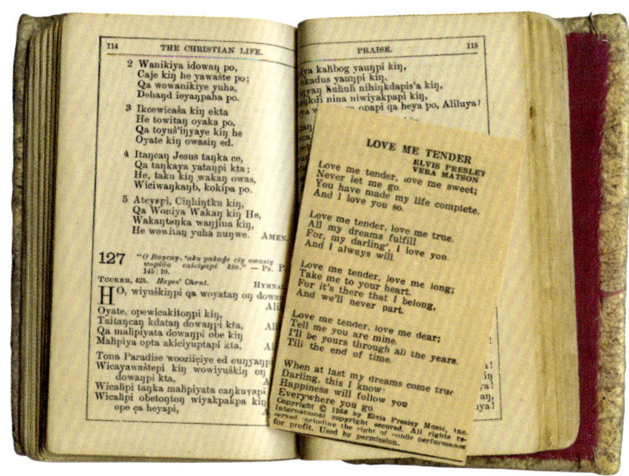

ELLEN HOLLOW HEAD'S LAKOTA AND ENGLISH HYMNAL, WITH "LOVE ME TENDER" BOOKMARK BY ELVIS.

with such a strong oral tradition, I saw that even as the details may differ from here to there, the ritual always comes from the heart, and the actions are done with sincerity, since the intended essence of the ritual is the same.

Participation in rituals and following the Good Red Road, as the spiritual path of the Lakota is known, is believed to strengthen the Sacred Hoop of Life. Traditionally, actions are not only done among Lakota to help only those in the current moment; rather, time is viewed as a continuum of past, present, and future, all having equal importance and affecting the sacred hoop of all living things. Each action is viewed in this way, considering its respect for the past, potential effect on the present, and imprint on future generations.

The most important feeling I wish to convey is the peaceful admiration I have felt in the company of Lakota friends. We have had wonderful conversations in which we discussed and, at times, even debated history, politics, and values. Life is not about the specific acts or spiritual practices that individuals or groups live by; rather, it is about the importance of acting from a truly positive and heartfelt place. These memories and influences from this shared time will live on, and I am so appreciative to have been touched by the manner of the Lakota people.

During one of the last conversations we had together, Grandfather Eugene asked how I would use the photographs I had made of his family and friends. I told him I expected they would only be mementos for his family, friends, and me to keep. He asked that I try to find a way to use them that might help his family and people.

I have since taken opportunities to donate photographs to the tribal archive and sell or publish prints as a means to raise funds for Lakota families and organizations. The photographs I made for this book and the compilation of other text, images, poems, and music that accompanies them are an attempt to bring this work to a point where it may have the kind of value Grandfather Eugene envisioned. Thus, just as I donated my royalties from the original (2010) edition of this book to KILI radio, so, too, am I donating my royalties for this new edition to "The Voice of the Lakota Nation." May this book, in its own small way, help draw additional support for KILI and the good work it does for the tribe. Even as *Views from the Reservation: A New Edition* may only scratch the surface of Lakota land and life and the challenging circumstances the Lakota people face, it is also a celebration and an appreciation of the positive and enduring elements of Lakota culture and native ground.

In closing, I am reminded of a quote by Lila Watson, an Australian aborigine: "If you have come to help me, you are wasting your time. But if you have come here because your liberation is bound up with mine, then let us work together." My relationship with the Lakota people does not end here, and my work is not finished. I will continue to return to Pine Ridge as long as I am able.

PLAYGROUND, OGLALA.

TIM KELLEY (LEFT) AND "OLD MAN" WILBUR MORRISON (CENTER) PREPARE FOR AN *INIPI* CEREMONY. USED BY PERMISSION.

Mitakuye Oyasin (Closing Prayer)

In honor of the seven Lakota nations and all other indigenous people of the world—from past, present, and future generations—I share these concluding thoughts:

Your traditional ways and respect for all living things and your valuing the interconnected relationship of all things are deserving of our respect and appreciation. There is no doubt the world will be a better place every moment we are able to live the ideals represented by the words *mitakuye oyasin*. The four sacred colors—red, yellow, white, and black—of the sacred medicine wheel represent the four directions—north, east, south, and west—in which all races of people come together, creating the Sacred Hoop of life. When people follow the Good Red Road and treat each other and all living things as part of this Sacred Hoop, we strengthen the Circle of Life (*Maka Wiconi*) for all generations.

Heartfelt regards and deep appreciation are sent to each and every one of you for every effort you put forth with mindfulness.

Mitakuye Oyasin
John Willis

TIN TEPEE, PINE RIDGE.

Notes on Selected Plates

Note to the Reader: With respect to Lakota tradition, no photographs were taken for this book during any sacred ceremony, and permissions were secured for the images taken before and after a ceremony. Also, the notes for the ledger art (on pages 84 and 121–28) were provided by the artist, Dwayne Wilcox, and the notes for pages 79 and 90–91 by Doyla Lundstrom.

PAGE 1. Leroy was born in this traditional log cabin at Lost Dog Creek more than sixty-five years ago, and he still lived in it when I took this photograph. The cabin is large enough to include a double-size bed, wood-burning stove, small chair, table, and television.

PAGE 10. The young Lakota riders are following another heat of riders at the Batesland Race Day, part of the Fourth of July Powwow. As the riders follow they call back in relay fashion to the spectators, who cannot always see the race over the rolling prairie. The title of the photograph (in Lakota) shares the same name as the nonprofit group that offers traditional teachings and experiences such as horseback riding and racing, camping, and archery to Lakota youth.

PAGE 14. This panoramic New Deal mural was painted by Andrew Standing as part of the Works Progress Administration (WPA) of the 1930s. It chronicles the history of the Pine Ridge Agency and encircles the walls of the auditorium in Pine Ridge High School. The mural dates from the days when the U.S. government still chose to send native youth to English-speaking boarding schools throughout the nation rather than have them attend a community public school immersed in the Lakota language and traditions. The youth would be shipped to reservations far enough away from their people to make it easier to require them to live without wearing traditional clothes, speaking their language, or practicing their religion. The school's student body would consist of members from many tribes, making it more difficult for the youth to hold on to their respective culture. The federal goal was to make Indian youth assimilate into mainstream society. These schools operated in this fashion from the late-nineteenth century into the 1960 and 70s. This mural was being removed from the school in the summer of 2004 but not because it was offensive; rather, the community took down the auditorium to build a more structurally sound one.

PAGE 22. Once I was with Tommy when he was paying his bill at the electric company, and he was given a calendar called "The American West." It was full of color illustrations of cowboys on the Great Plains. Tommy laughed and called it *Wasichu Weocpayata* (The White Man's West).

PAGE 23. Many native people also complain about Crazy Horse Mountain being sculpted in the same sacred Black Hills (*Paha Sapa*), since the act of carving into these sacred mountains by anyone is unacceptable. Still, the historical policies against American Indians by the U.S. government, including the four presidents represented on Mount Rushmore, remain deep concerns for native people even today. President Barack Obama, however, had good relations with America's indigenous nations. His activism and leadership, especially at Bears Ears and Standing Rock, were much appreciated by native people everywhere.

PAGE 26. Some have commented that this image is metaphorically representative of the bison alone on the Great Plains, where once there were millions. As that may be true, the lone bull here has been outcast from the herd by a stronger and more dominant bull.

PAGE 29. For twenty generations and counting, all *c'anupas* (also spelled *cannupa* and *channupa*), the sacred pipe central to Lakota ceremony, have been made of red (catlinite) pipestone rock mined in the same location in Pipestone, Minnesota. The word is probably made from the compounds "can" (pronounced chan), meaning "tree," and "unpa," meaning "to smoke." Smoking the pipe in the proper ritualistic fashion sends one's prayers to the Great Spirit in the *cansasa* smoking mixture made of special herbs. Black Elk (*Heháka Sápa*), the famous medicine and holy man (*wicháša wakhán*) and šacred clown (*heyókha*) of the Oglala Lakota (b. 1863; d. 1950), is attributed for saying, "When you pray with this pipe, you pray for and with everything." Carrying a pipe requires a commitment to live in a sacred manner. Doing so properly means that one will contribute to the strength of the Sacred Hoop of all people from past, present, and future generations who walk the Good Red Road. Not caring for one's pipe properly or not living in a sacred manner would correspondingly weaken the hoop, harming not only the pipe carrier, but also all of his or her relations. These relations are not only blood relations, but also all who have chosen to live on the Good Red Road.

PAGES 32 AND 34. *Tinpsila* (also spelled *timpsula)*, a wild prairie turnip (*Pediomelum esculenta*), at one time was one of the most important foods gathered by the Lakota and other Great Plains tribes. The root can be eaten raw, cooked in *wahampi* (soups), or made into a flour. Lewis and Clark wrote of the Lakota collecting, peeling, and frying these "white apples."

Pages 40 and 41. Joseph M. Marshall, III, the acclaimed author of *The Lakota Way: Stories and Lessons for Living* (2001) and other books who was born and raised on the Rosebud Lakota (*Sicangu*) Reservation, speaks of "the circle" (*kaohomni*, pronounced *ga-oh-ho-mnee*) as being an essential element and icon in traditional Lakota life, because—like the four seasons—life itself moves in cycles (thus circles). The longstanding traditional design of conical dwellings (the tepee, which means "they live there"), religious ceremonies (including the *inipi* or sweat lodge), and group lodging was a practical and spiritual application of the circle. When nomadic life was still possible and the seven Lakota nations depended on the bison roaming free—that is, before the bison population was decimated by Euro-Americans and before the "reservation" limited and defined Lakota "territories" and the Lakota way of life—tepees were arranged in circular villages or encampments, with all entrances for doorways and villages alike facing east toward the sunrise and away from the harsh westerly and northwesterly winds of winter. Government housing on the reservation today does not conform to the circle. Instead, homes are rectangular or square, and they are often lined up in rows or clusters, like a subdivision. Their entrances are also just as likely to face west or north or south as they are the traditional (that is, the practical and spiritual) east. There is now talk of trying to reintroduce the circle into future architectural renderings.

page 62. Under the Fort Laramie Treaty of 1868, the U.S. government mandated that it would provide food to the Lakota people, if they lived on the reservations. The government's food allotment has been delivered in the form of monthly commodities. Prior to the change in diet created by the commodity program, the Lakota ate a natural diet high in protein and low in unhealthy fats. Since becoming accustomed to the commodity diet, their health has been dramatically affected with extremely high rates of obesity, diabetes, and heart disease. In recent years, the Lakota people and federal government have been making a concerted effort to improve the nutritional quality of the commodities. Where some racists viewed the program as the Lakota freeloading off the government, the Lakota at times viewed it as induced poisoning. The issues raised by the commodities program are similar to issues around the Indian Health Service, also mandated in the Fort Laramie Treaty. The medical practitioners do their best but are constantly fighting against poor preventive practices and cuts to the budget. It is all too common to learn of needed treatments being turned down or patients being sent home from hospitals and clinics earlier than their condition would typically suggest for non-native patients.

PAGE 63. The condition of this car is a common sight to see on the reservation. Tribal police have jurisdiction throughout the reservation. I have never heard of them citing someone for driving any operable vehicle on the reservation, while it is common knowledge that many of the same vehicles would be pulled over by non-tribal police as soon as the vehicles leave the reservation roads. The tribal police are far more forgiving, because they know the extreme poverty and needs of residents to get from country homes to and fro for health, food, education, and all-too-rare work needs.

PAGE 64. John F. Kennedy and Robert F. Kennedy both visited Pine Ridge Reservation. They were instrumental in the building of government housing. Prior to their visits, many Lakota still lived in tents or at best small log homes. The HUD (Housing and Urban Development) program has been building housing clusters. Increasing the number and size of homes has improved reservation lifestyle but also presents problems. Since firewood and water are not abundant in the Great Plains, cluster housing does not always fare well with poor and unemployed people surviving off the land.

PAGE 71. During the Fourth of July powwow, the nonprofit *Sunka Wakan Na Wakanyeja Awicaglipi* (To Bring Back the Horse and Child) helped to sponsor youth riders in community races. The group also raises funds and sponsors youth on memorial rides such as the Big Foot Ride and Crazy Horse Ride.

PAGE 73. During a cold winter day, just after Christmas in 1890, an estimated 250–300 Mniconju (Minnecojou) Lakota women, children, and braves led by Chief Big Foot were massacred and wounded at this site at Wounded Knee. It was one of the last "battles" between the Great Plains tribes and the U.S. government. According to Joseph M. Marshall, III, in his book, *The Lakota Way: Stories and Lessons for Living* (2001), Chief Big Foot and his band of 350 had been living along the Cheyenne River in north-central South Dakota and had been invited by Chief Red Cloud to come to the Pine Ridge Reservation. The U.S. Seventh Cavalry, along with the Ninth Cavalry—the famed "Negro Unit" known as the Buffalo

Soldiers—intercepted Chief Big Foot and his band about thirty miles east of the reservation, at which point he surrendered. The Indians were then escorted in the harsh winter weather to Wounded Knee Creek, where the captors decided to search and take away the Indians' last few remaining weapons, which they had been told they could keep for hunting and survival. A struggle broke out when one elderly brave did not want to give up his rifle. It is believed the rifle went off accidentally in the commotion. The nearly 500 soldiers, who had surrounded the Lakota camp the night before, then opened fire—including the use of rapid-fire, light-artillery Hotchkiss guns—on the band of mostly unarmed captives. The next day, the bodies were gathered up from a distance of three miles, where they had been slaughtered as they ran. The soldiers buried 146 of them in one mass grave at this site. Later, a monument was placed here to honor those killed. The soldiers received twenty Congressional Medals of Honor from a grateful government for their efforts.

In 1973, the site was chosen by the American Indian Movement (AIM) for an occupation to protest the treatment of native peoples. Several hundred people took over the site and demanded there be an investigation into the practices of the Bureau of Indian Affairs, the government agency managing native issues. The protestors came from sixty-four different tribes. They were surrounded by U.S. marshals, F.B.I. agents, the National Guard, and other paramilitary groups. A siege took place, which lasted seventy-one days. During that time, 133,000 rounds of ammunition were used against the protestors, and roadblocks were placed everywhere to keep food, medical supplies, military gear, ammunition, and other items from being delivered into the occupation. Fifty-one percent of American people were said to have sympathized with the natives, while only twenty-one percent disagreed. The government was finally able to end the occupation by promising amnesty for everyone and agreeing to open talks regarding their concerns. Neither of those promises has been kept. Nonetheless, as Vine Deloria, Jr., revealed in his pathbreaking book, *God Is Red: A Native View of Religion* (1973, 1992, and 2003), "through all the protests and symbolic gestures, a different sense of Indian identity was born" (page 20). This is the same gravesite Kent Nerburn writes about in his essay (on pages 93–94).

PAGE 76. The owner of these tepees was a Vietnam War veteran who reminded me that flying the Amercan flag upside-down is a signal of dire distress. He said he displayed the union down when the George W. Bush administration started treating Muslims with the same bigoted practices the government had long used against American Indians.

PAGE 79. Brett Lee Lundstrom was born on June 12, 1983, in Vermillion, South Dakota,where his parents, Doyla and Ed, attended the University of South Dakota. After graduation, Ed joined the U.S. Marine Corps, and so Brett was influenced by his father and a military life dedicated to honor and service. Brett was attending college in New Jersey and was enrolled in a Marine Officer Candidate Program when 9/11 occurred. He withdrew and enlisted in the Marine Corps, believing his service was needed on behalf of his nation. His first deployment was to Afghanistan in 2004. His second deployment in 2005 was to Fallujah, Iraq, where he was killed in action on January 7, 2006.

PAGE 80. In the old days, especially before the automobile, there was one Sun Dance each year, and it served both the Pine Ridge and Rosebud Reservations. Today, with increasing participation in this cultural and spiritual practice, there are as many as eighty Sun Dances each year on the Pine Ridge Reservation alone. When a family decides to host a Sun Dance, the family is making a very large commitment of work and finances, and a Sun Dance leader and a medicine man are needed to help run the ceremony. As with many native rituals that rely on the number four, the commitment is for a cycle of four consecutive years, which represent the four directions and four seasons. Each Sun Dance during this cycle is held at the same location, although the shade arbor, sweat lodges, and other structures are usually reconstructed each year. A new cottonwood tree also needs to be harvested each year for the four-day ceremony, in which dancers take no food or water. The site is carefully selected in order to provide a beautiful setting in which to commune with *Maka Takiya* (Grandmother Earth) during the ritual of prayer as well as to offer security from unwanted visitors.

PAGE 84. Thank God the Christians came to this country and straightened us out.

PAGES 90–91. Brett Lundstrom was the only Oglala Lakota to lose his life in the Iraq conflict. Upon learning of his passing, the community of the Pine Ridge Reservation responded with a tremendous outpouring of love and honor for Brett's life. People came from great distances. He was given a true warrior's service, with Brett lying in state in a tepee and the Marine Corps standing at attention for the days of services and the wake. Children, adults, and elders of the Oglala Lakota Tribe came in respect of the ultimate sacrifice any Oglala warrior would ever make. Brett's memory and sacrifice are well remembered on the Pine Ridge Reservation. When his name is mentioned, you see a mixture of pride and sadness for the brave young Lakota warrior who died serving his country and defending a way of life. He was laid to rest at Fort Logan National Cemetery in Denver, Colorado.

PAGE 108. Each housing community on the reservation has water towers required to ensure there is enough water for that community. This always reminds me how the U.S. government allocated as permanent reservation land those lands throughout the country which it felt were the least desirable and would stay that way, not realizing at the time that these types of terrain also are where some of the nations's most valuable mineral deposits exist. Disputes over such lands have existed ever since. The Oglala Lakota people had their sacred Black Hills (*Paha Sapa*), which were given to them in the second Fort Laramie Treaty of 1868 and were subsequently stolen back from them, when gold was discovered. After many years of fighting in court for their land rights to the Black Hills, the U.S. Supreme Court in 1980 ruled in the tribe's favor. During the legal battle, so much time had passed with individuals and businesses purchasing and developing the land that the Court decided the Lakota people could not return to the land, which was wrongfully taken. A cash settlement was offered instead. The native people would not accept cash for their most sacred land. The outcome? More than $1,000,000,000 is sitting in escrow for the tribe to accept as payment in exchange for their land. To this date, the tribe has chosen not to do so on principle, while the people live in the poorest conditions of the most powerful nation in the world. Still, the Lakota belief structure and spirituality for this generation and those to come are too important to the people to give up for financial gain.

PAGE 110. I grew up in Connecticut, where family members and mourners in a traditional graveside funeral leave before the gravediggers come out of the shadows to fill in the grave. Here, members of the Swift Hawk family, predominately the sons and grandsons, fill the grave with soil as quickly as they physically can. Sun Dance singers in the background drum and sing sacred songs, while Leonard Crow Dog, a medicine man, offers prayers. Supporters who have come to honor Grandfather Earl and his family stand and pray as the gravesite is filled. All is done in a sacred manner to assist Earl's spirit in leaving for the journey to the spirit world.

PAGE 121. Fort Robinson, in the Pine Ridge country of northwestern Nebraska, is where Crazy Horse (*Tȟašúnke Witkó*) was incarcerated and murdered in 1877 at age thirty-six or thirty-seven. I began to wonder, What if the Cheyenne and Lakota people took over the place? Since many

Indians were imprisoned here and elsewhere for refusing to give up their right to be free, many of the earliest ledgers were done during their imprisonment.

PAGE 122. Some non-natives are a little too energetic about seeing natives in dance regalia at urban powwows. Sometimes they go a little overboard on the camera action. After these events, no one is waiting outside when they come out in their everyday clothes.

PAGE 123. The U.S. government still believes that all the treaties made with the Lakota people are old news, and anything about them is just whining. This is the reward for being a good Indian for more than 100 years of food subsidies, no employment, poverty, and for living in one of America's poorest counties.

PAGE 124. Imagine having a different view from time to time instead of having a summer home, a winter home, and a vacation home that you have to pay utilities on year-round. Talk about going green.

PAGE 125. President Reagan, in a different time, would have called the soldiers "freedom fighters," if America wasn't the aggressor. Lakotas fought against this country and then for this country, from World War I to this day. We continue to give our lives for America.

PAGE 126. Sometimes the only horse you can get is the one you have to rent.

PAGE 127. *Wash' tay* in Lakota means "good." Yes, we stay in tepees from time to time: during the Sun Dance, some powwows, some protests, or in the summer when it is too hot in the house.

PAGE 128. A culture under the microscope from every angle, outsiders come to pry and pray to a government that believes it knows what is best for native people: They knew that from the start. Every white man or woman with a Ph.D. in American Indian history or M.D. in public health gets the freedom to write a book or research paper about the people he or she studied. Health studies cover the plight of a certain group of people with specific indigenous issues. Movie makers come and wish we all still live in tepees, and the absurd storylines always end with the great white man saving the day. And then there are those who come to find a native man or woman to marry and have more mixed-blood children like me.

Sorry to disappoint so many that I don't look Indian enough for you, and thanks for telling me that so freely. Sometimes you need to keep those inner thoughts to yourself. I grew up on a reservation, and I personally know exactly what an Indian looks like, and as an adult I've seen my reflection in a mirror.

PAGES 180, 182, 184, AND 186. As I travel across the country and internationally, I am struck by the pervasiveness of economic inequality—a condition that seems to be worsening. Since 1992 I have closely observed the people of the Pine Ridge Reservation in South Dakota and more recently the Navajo Nation in Arizona. I am deeply troubled by the injustices experienced by indigenous tribes. I was inspired to begin creating work for this series on reservation housing in an effort to document an appalling act perpetrated by the U.S. government upon its own citizens. In the aftermath of Hurricane Katrina (2005), the Federal Emergency Management Agency (FEMA) sent prefabricated trailers to New Orleans to replace lost housing. The units later proved to contain toxic levels of formaldehyde and were deemed too poisonous for habitation. FEMA reclaimed the trailers and sold them to Native Americans, including Oglala Lakota families on the Pine Ridge Reservation, for $3,000 each—the cost of shipping. Such false charity recalls a litany of abuses heaped upon Native Americans for centuries. These four images are from a larger body of work that is meant to draw attention to the plight of native people in the United States and how their circumstances reflect the hypocrisy and poor ethical choices of our society. I encourage viewers to consider these images as a metaphor for the nation and to engage in a dialogue about the values we claim to uphold and what they really mean.

AMERICAN HORSE ROAD.

List of Poems

* She or he was a high-school student from the Pine Ridge Reservation at the time the poem was written. All poems in the book are used by permission and may not be reproduced without written approval of the poet, student, or elder.

TRAILER HOME WITH ROOF BLOWN OFF,
AMERICAN HORSE ROAD.

List of Songs from *Heartbeat of the Rez*

TRACK 1	*Opening Prayer for His Friends*	Eugene Reddest
TRACK 2	*KILI Radio Song*	Chris Eagle Hawk
TRACK 3	*The Owl Told Me*	Everett Lone Hill
TRACK 4	*Encouragement Song*	John Around Him
TRACK 5	*Soldier's Ceremony Song*	John Around Him
TRACK 6	*Powwow Song*	Chris Eagle Hawk
TRACK 7	*Rabbit Dance*	Will Peters
TRACK 8	*Four Directions Song*	Quincy Red Feather
TRACK 9	Wakan Tanka Unsimala	Last Horse Family
TRACK 10	*Veteran's Song* (live at KILI Radio)	Jake Arapahoe, Chubb White Mouse, and Wilbur Morrison
TRACK 11	Maya Aninhpe Wiwarg Wacipi Olawar	Last Horse Family
TRACK 12	*Sun Dance Song*	Last Horse Family
TRACK 13	C'anupe Olawan	David Swallow, Jr., and Nyla Helper
TRACK 14	*Forgiveness*	David Swallow, Jr., and Nyla Helper
TRACK 15	Wocekiya Olawan	David Swallow, Jr., and Nyla Helper
TRACK 16	Wopila *Song*	David Swallow, Jr., and Nyla Helper
TRACK 17	*Native Thang*	Cy Patton and Derrick Janis
TRACK 18	*A Reservation Tale*	Cy Patton and Derrick Janis
TRACK 19	*Who We Are*	Cy Patton and Derrick Janis, in addition to Featuring Native Empire, Sundown Montileaure, Clay Janis, and Hawkeye Montileaux
TRACK 20	*Listening/Honor Song*	John Trudell

The original (2010) edition of this book included a CD entitled *Heartbeat of the Rez*. It was a *wopila* (gift) for the Lakota people and was compiled by John Willis and mastered by Bill Esses, of Brattleboro, Vermont. To access the CD, visit *www.jwillis.net*. All songs used by permission. Tracks 1–7 are from the KILI 25th Anniversary CD; tracks 3–16 are *inipi* (sweat lodge) songs; tracks 17–19 appear courtesy of District Records, of Washington, D.C.; and Track 20 is from *Tribal Voice* by John Trudell (cassette, 1983; CD, 2003). The cover artwork for the CD by Derrick Jannis (© 2010) appears opposite page 192 on the inside of the end-sheet and is used by permission.

BIA ROUTE 118, PINE RIDGE.

About the Craft

The development of this book has spanned nearly three decades. Within that timeframe, I have used a wide range of camera formats, from 35mm to 8 × 10 inch view cameras, from analog processes to digital technology. Each offers its own benefits.

While the photographic medium's technology and craftsmanship have always been a joy to work with, neither has been the essence of what photography is about for me. I benefit from the experience of learning from and sharing with subjects while considering the world around us. Thus, a core goal within the process of making photographs on the reservation has been to find ways of connecting with the people, photographing with their permission, not being invasive, and having a relationship with them, which helps me as an outsider attempting to understand Lakota heritage and the everyday circumstances that the Lakota people are living with in a meaningful and open-minded way.

When editing and compiling both the original (2010) and new (2019) editions of the book, I had many exchanges and made multiple trips to show the photographs and the evolving book with the community and its elders, leaders, teachers, and everyday people. I would sit and ask what they thought, what did and did not work, and what needed to be included, added, or left out—always with the consciousness it would be impossible to please everyone. Nonetheless, I am grateful I was able to share the photographs and to secure the permissions to reproduce them. I/we related to the project as a mosaic of information with the thought that, if people read the whole book, they will feel the effort was worthy. I can only hope that is true.

I learn from my subjects and hope that the relationship we create, whether for one moment or years, will be beneficial to us all. Although it might be easier to be satisfied making work only about what I know and live personally, I long for the connection to others, which usually broadens my horizons and belief structures. Maybe by sharing the outsider/insider relationship within the process and consciously questioning it with subjects as viewers, there may be more positive effect than not. At least that is an ongoing goal in my personal photographic work and in the work and teaching I do at Marlboro College and with two non-profit organizations that I co-founded: the In-Sight Photography Project (www.insight-photography.org) and Exposures (www.exposuresprogram.org).

NO FLESH ROAD.

Acknowledgments

There are so many people on the Pine Ridge Reservation whom I wish to thank and acknowledge for the years of sharing and assisting with this project. I've made sincere good-faith efforts to share the contents of the book as it evolved with the Lakota people, including all the subjects and contributors. For those whom I have been unable to sit and share the project with as it unfolded, I can only hope you will appreciate the book and its goals. I offer special thanks to Andrea Marshall and the Reddest Family, Alma Richards and Leonard Black Cat, Wendell and Delores Yellow Bull, Melanie and Derrick Janis, Wilbur Morrison, Chubb and Marian White Mouse, Quincy Red Feather, Jake Arapahoe, Karen Weasel Bear, Chic Big Crow, Matt Rama, Tom Casey, and Gerard Baker. I also thank the book's contributors, including the writers, students, curators, musicians, subjects in the photographs, and all Lakota people who have been so welcoming to me. My sincerest love and appreciation also go out to my wife, Pauline Brett, whom I met in Eugene's house on the Pine Ridge Reservation, and to my son, Elijah, for their continued support.

With gratitude I acknowledge that this book has been made possible with the generous support of George F. Thompson, who helped me develop, sequence, and publish both the original (2010) and new (2019) editions, as well as David Skolkin, book designer for both editions, Diane Boehm, Lindy Linder, Ray A. Graham, III, Richard S. and Jeanne Press, Ralph and Nancy Segall, Harry and Irina Brandler, Gisela and David Gamper, Peggy Farber, Jo Ann Eder, George Miles, Yale University's Beinecke Collection, Marlboro College, the Vermont Arts Council, the Vermont Arts Endowment, the National Endowment for the Arts, and Lillian Farber and Bern Friedelson. And many others have been inspirational and given help to this project, too many to list here, but they include Jane Winterling, Erin Barnard, the staff and participants of the Exposures Cross Cultural Youth Program, in addition to Martha A. Sandweiss, Jim Cortez, Don Hutchinson, Sarah Danner, Deb Tobacco and Oglala Lakota College, Jerry Swope, John Sheehy, Tim Kelly, Meta Willis, David P. Willis, Alan Willis, Faye Brown, and John Trudell, whose book of poems, *Lines from a Mined Mind: The Words of John Trudell*, was published in 2008 by Fulcrum Publishing.

To everyone listed here and to those I have unintentionally not mentioned, I am deeply indebted and grateful to you.

About the Essayist

Kent Nerburn was born and raised in Minnesota. He received his B.A. in American studies, summa cum laude, from the University of Minnesota and his Ph.D. in theology, with distinction, from the Graduate Theological Union and University of California, Berkeley. Nerburn has been praised as "one of the few American writers who can respectfully bridge the gap between native and non-native cultures." He is the author of sixteen books of creative nonfiction and essays focusing on spiritual values and American Indian culture, including *Voices in the Stones: Life Lessons from the Native Way* (2016), *The Girl Who Sang to the Buffalo: A Child, an Elder, and the Light from an Ancient Sky* (2013), *The Wolf of Twilight: An Indian Elder's Journey through a Land of Ghosts and Shadows* (2009), and *Neither Wolf nor Dog: On Forgotten Roads with an Indian Elder* (1994), all published by New World Library. The latter was cited by the American Indian College Fund as "one of those rare works that, once you've read it, you can never look at the world, or at people, the same way again" and was adapted into an acclaimed movie in 2017. His historical narrative, *Chief Joseph and the Flight of the Nez Perce: The Untold Story of an American Tragedy* (HarperCollins, 2005), was called by Nez Perce elders "the one account that addresses the whole story of the flight of the Nez Perce" and praised by novelist Louise Erdrich as "storytelling with a greatness of heart." Nerburn has also compiled several anthologies of Native American thought, including *The Wisdom of the Native Americans* (New World Library, 1996) and *The Wisdom of the Native Americans* (New World Library, 1999), and produced an updated version of *The Soul of an Indian*, Ohiyesa's (Charles Alexander Eastman's) classic exploration of Dakota spirituality and values. Nerburn has appeared on C-Span and the History Channel, has spoken at many universities, tribal colleges, and other organizations in America and abroad, and served on the advisory board of Red Feather Development Group, a nonprofit organization that assists tribes in building straw-bale housing on reservations. Nerburn makes his home with his wife outside Portland, Oregon. His Website is www.kentnerburn.com.

About the Author

John Willis was born and raised in Stamford, Connecticut. After receiving his M.F.A. in photography from the Rhode Island School of Design in 1986, he joined Marlboro College, where he is a professor of photography. He is also the co-founder of the In-Sight Photography Project (www.insight-photography.org), which offers courses to the youth of southern Vermont regardless of their ability to pay, and the Exposures Cross Cultural Youth Photography Program (www.exposures-program.com), which brings youth together from a wide variety of backgrounds to share photography lessons and life stories. Following the publication of *Views from the Reservation* he was awarded a John Simon Guggenheim Memorial Foundation Fellowship in Photography. He has also received numerous artist fellowships from the Vermont Council on the Arts and Vermont Art Endowment. His photographs are in more than sixty collections, including the Amon Carter Museum, Bibliothèque Nationale de France, Center for Creative Photography, George Eastman House International Museum of Photography and Film, J. Paul Getty Museum, High Museum of Art, Library of Congress, Museum of Fine Arts, Boston, Museum of Fine Arts, Houston, National Gallery of Art, National Museum of the American Indian, Nelson-Adkins Museum of Arts, Portland (Oregon) Museum of Art, Princeton University Art Museum, San Francisco Museum of Modern Art, Tokyo Metropolitan Museum of Photography, Whitney Museum of American Art, and Yale University Gallery of Art. His photographs have been exhibited nationally and internationally, including solo exhibitions at the Stark Gallery in New York City, Blue Sky Gallery in Portland, Oregon, Oglala Lakota College in Kyle, South Dakota, Photographic Resource Center in Boston, and Robert F. Fullerton Museum in San Bernardino, California. His photographs have been featured in various published books and journals, including *LensWork*, *Orion*, and *Flesh and Blood: Photographers' Images of Their Own Families*, published by the Picture Project. Willis's other books are *Recycled Realities*, a collaborative effort with photographer Tom Young (Center for American Places, 2005), and *Mni Wiconi: Honoring the Water Protectors at Standing Rock and Elsewhere in the Ongoing Struggle for Indigenous Sovereignty* (George F. Thompson Publishing, 2019). His Website is www.jwillis.net.

About the Book

Views from the Reservation was first published as the eighteenth volume in the *Center Books on American Places* series, George F. Thompson, series founder and director. That original edition was brought to publication in 2010 by the Center for American Places at Columbia College Chicago in an edition of 1,750 hardcover copies. This updated and expanded new edition was brought to publication in an edition of 1,250 hardcover copies with the generous support of Richard S. and Jeanne Press, Ralph and Nancy Segall, Harry and Irina Brandler, and Diane Boehm, for which the publisher and author are most grateful. The text was set in Minion, the paper is Gold East matte art, 170 gsm weight, and the book was professionally printed and bound by TWP in Malaysia.

Editorial note: The definition of reservation (on page 9) is derived, in part, from *The Oxford American College Dictionary* (New York: G. P. Putnam's Sons, 2002), 1152, and *Merriam-Webster's Collegiate Dictionary*, Tenth Edition (Springfield, MA: Merriam-Webster, 2002), 993.

Project Director and Publisher: George F. Thompson
Editorial and Research Assistant: Mikki Soroczak
Manuscript Editor: Purna Makaram
Production Assistant: Michael Motley
Book Designer and Production: David Skolkin

Coda

I am often asked, "What has changed since *Views from the Reservation* was first published in 2010?" Based on what I have heard and seen in my ongoing annual visits and extensive time spent on the Pine Ridge and other Lakota reservations, life has not become easier.

Under President Barack Obama, there was hope for a better future. He listened to and respected the views of America's indigenous people and brought them to the table as few American presidents had before. Witness his moratorium and temporary stoppage of the Dakota Access Pipeline (DAPL) from entering the burial grounds and other sacred lands of the Standing Rock Lakota Tribe; witness his protection of 1,350,000 acres of sacred Indian land in Utah with his declaration of Bears Ears National Monument, in which native people were involved, for the first time, in the establishment and management of federal lands.

And then came President Donald J. Trump and a return to the dark ages of American history. Witness his support of DAPL's location and infringement on the sovereignty of the Standing Rock Lakota Tribe; witness his unprecedented reduction of Bears Ears National Monument to 221,000 acres; witness his acceptance of the actions and rants of neo-Nazis and white supremacists at Charlottesville and elsewhere; witness his denigration of survivors of sexual abuse and his overall demeanor toward foreigners and people of color. Native friends are seriously worried about what this man and his base are capable of doing.

As long as I can remember, federal and state governments always claim that changes in various policies will not negatively affect low-income and poor Americans. My native friends often speak about their community being so economically challenged that they barely notice the differences between the so-called "good" and "bad" economic times. But, under President Trump, there has been a worrisome and devastating return to policies and declarations that cause anguish, instill fear, and cause hurt and harm to native people of all ages and abilities.

The need to raise awareness regarding the ways that racist practices and government-inflicted injustices affect America's indigenous peoples and all underprivileged people seems as strong now as ever. That is what I hear and see every time I am on the reservation. It is time we do our part to help change perceptions and understandings of Lakota land and life by outsiders.

Published in 2019.
Printed in Malaysia on acid-free paper.

George F. Thompson Publishing, L.L.C.
217 Oak Ridge Circle
Staunton, VA 24401–3511, U.S.A.
www.gftbooks.com

27 26 25 24 23 22 21 20 19 1 2 3 4 5

The Library of Congress Preassigned Control Number is 2018910673.

ISBN: 978–1–938086–63–2

HEARTBEAT

OF THE REZ

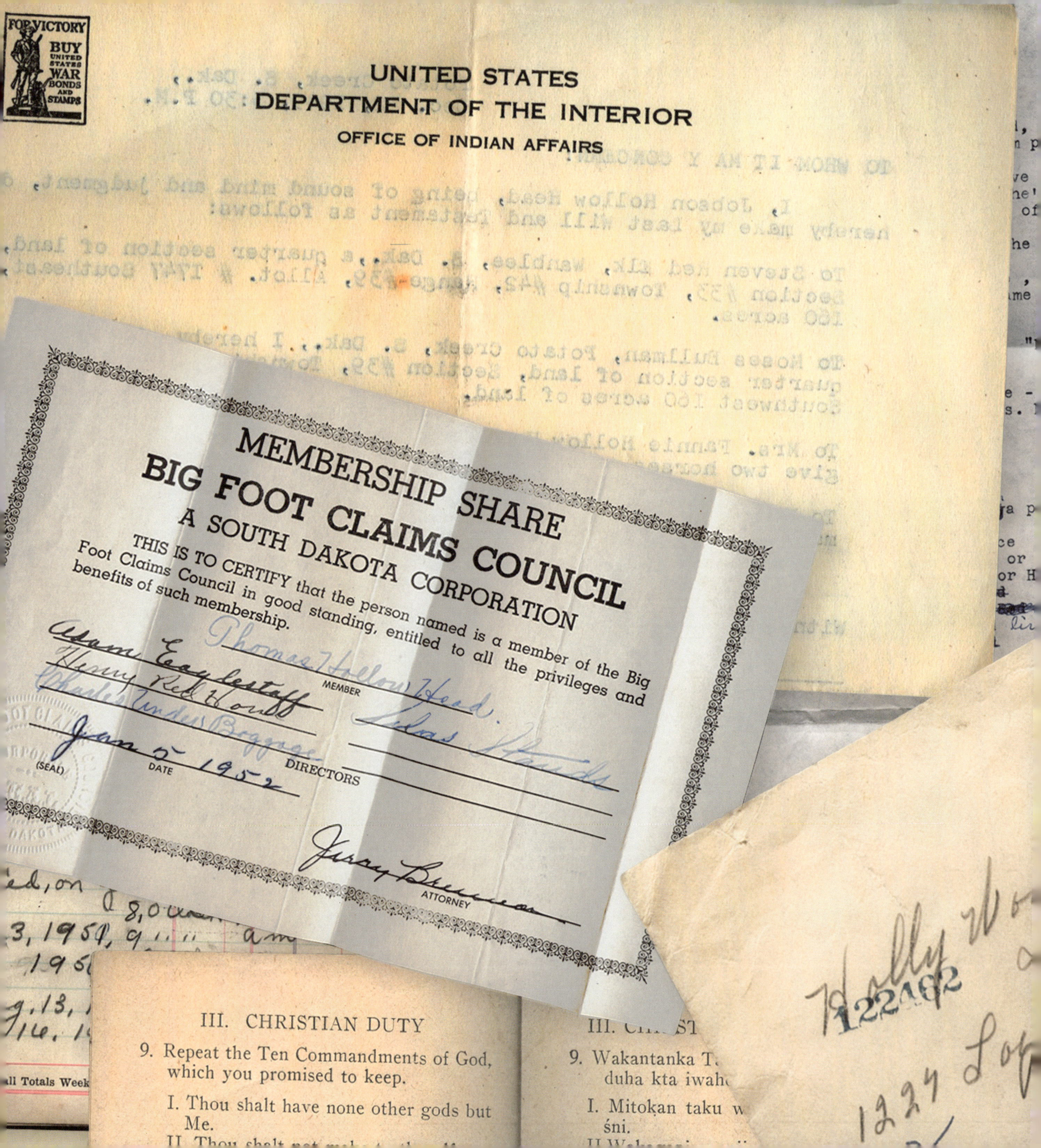

UNITED STATES
DEPARTMENT OF THE INTERIOR
OFFICE OF INDIAN AFFAIRS

MEMBERSHIP SHARE
BIG FOOT CLAIMS COUNCIL
A SOUTH DAKOTA CORPORATION

THIS IS TO CERTIFY that the person named is a member of the Big Foot Claims Council in good standing, entitled to all the privileges and benefits of such membership.

Thomas Hollow Head.
MEMBER

Adam Eaglestaff
Henry Red Horse
Charles Under Baggage
Silas Stands
DIRECTORS

(SEAL)

Jan 5 1952
DATE

ATTORNEY

III. CHRISTIAN DUTY

9. Repeat the Ten Commandments of God, which you promised to keep.

I. Thou shalt have none other gods but Me.

III. CHRIST

9. Wakantanka T
duha kta iwah

I. Mitokan taku w
śni.